Quantum Human Design Evolution Guide

2026

Using Solar Transits to Design Your Year

Dr. Karen Parker

Copyright © 2025 by Dr. Karen Parker

2026 Quantum Human Design Evolution Guide

Using Solar Transits to Design Your Year

All rights reserved.

No part of this work may be used or reproduced, transmitted, stored, or used in any form or by any means graphic, electronic, or mechanical, including but not limited to photocopying, recording, scanning, digitizing, taping, Web distribution, information networks or information storage and retrieval systems, or in any manner whatsoever without prior written permission from the publisher.

Without in any way limiting the author's and publisher's exclusive rights under copyright, any use of this publication to train generative artificial intelligence (AI) or Large Language Model (LLM) technologies to generate text is expressly prohibited.

The content of this book is for informational purposes only and is not intended to diagnose, treat, cure, or prevent any condition or disease. You understand that this book is not intended as a substitute for consultation with a licensed practitioner. Please consult with your own physician or healthcare specialist regarding the suggestions and recommendations made in this book. The use of this book implies your acceptance of this disclaimer.

Edited by Melissa Rudder

Cover Design by Kristina Edstrom

HUMAN DESIGN PRESS

An Imprint for GracePoint Publishing (www.GracePointPublishing.com)

GracePoint Matrix, LLC

624 S. Cascade Ave, Suite 201, Colorado Springs, CO 80903

www.GracePointMatrix.com   Email: Admin@GracePointMatrix.com

SAN # 991-6032

A Library of Congress Control Number has been requested and is pending.

ISBN: (Paperback) 978-1-966346-44-9

eISBN: 978-1-966346-45-6

Books may be purchased for educational, business, or sales promotional use.

For non-retail bulk order requests contact Orders@GracePointPublishing.com

Printed in U.S.A

To all the conscious creators of the world—the ones who have risked everything to rest, to heal, and to remember who they truly are.

This book is for those brave enough to align their lives with authenticity, who know that the inner work is not separate from world work—it is the work.

May your courage to reclaim your truth, your willingness to reimagine what's possible, and your devotion to creating from integrity be the seeds of a world that is equitable, just, sustainable, abundant, and peaceful—for all.

Table of Contents

INTRODUCTION 6

HOW TO USE THIS BOOK 8

THE THEME OF THE YEAR 2026: THE YEAR OF CONSCIOUS CREATION 9

THE NODES 12

URANUS, NEPTUNE, AND PLUTO—THE OUTER PLANETS AND GLOBAL THEMES 17

SATURN AND JUPITER 19

2026 ECLIPSE SEASON 22

MY CHART 24

EVOLUTION GUIDE 45

    JANUARY 2026 46

    FEBRUARY 2026 50

    MARCH 2026 69

    APRIL 2026 87

    MAY 2026 103

    JUNE 2026 122

    JULY 2026 141

    AUGUST 2026 159

    SEPTEMBER 2026 175

    OCTOBER 2026 191

    NOVEMBER 2026 212

    DECEMBER 2026 228

    JANUARY 2027 246

SUMMARY 255

ABOUT THE AUTHOR 257

INTRODUCTION

This book is a weekly guide designed to give you a deliberate way to harness the energy of the Sun and the Moon to support you in creating what you want in your life.

Quantum Human Design is a collection of cross-cultural, ancient, and modern archetypes. An archetype is a pattern of thought or symbolic image that is derived from the past collective experience of humanity.

We experience all the archetypes in the Human Design charts, either from our own unique charts and relationships or through the planetary transits. In other words, we all have all of the chart. We just experience the archetypes of the chart differently depending on the unique configuration of our individual charts.

The colored in, or "defined," elements in your Human Design chart tell you which archetypes you carry. The defined elements are part of what you must conquer to bring your gifts into the world. These energies represent your soul curriculum, what you're here to learn over the course of your life, and what you must learn to love and accept about yourself.

The white, or "undefined," elements in your Human Design chart tell you a lot about what you are here to learn from others and from the world. You will experience these archetypes in a variety of ways depending on who you are with and what energies are transiting in the celestial weather. The themes you explore through your relationships with others and your interactions with the world are here to teach you how to self-regulate and hold on to your energy, no matter what's going on around you.

Over the course of a calendar year, the Sun moves through all 64 of the Human Design gates. The Human Design gates contain the energy code for 64 core human archetypes. As the Sun moves through an archetype, it "lights up" that theme for everyone on the planet for the week.

We all deal with the weekly themes. Even if the theme doesn't impact your chart deeply, it will impact the charts of the people around you. The gift of the solar transit is that it gives you an opportunity to work deliberately with all 64 of these core human archetypes and to consciously focus on living the highest expression of these energies in your daily life. The solar transit also brings you creative energies that help you meet the goals you set for yourself each year.

The Earth moves in partnership with the Sun, also changing gate themes every six days. The gates highlighted by the Earth represent what we need in order to ground ourselves. The energy of the Earth represents what we have to heal and allow in order to optimize the work the Sun's theme assigns us.

The Moon in Human Design represents the energy of what drives us. In traditional astrology, the new moon phase and the full moon phase represent bookend energies that mark the beginning and the end of a monthly creative cycle.

The new moon helps us set the intention for our goals for the month. The full moon supports us in releasing any energies, beliefs, or blocks that are hindering the completion of our goals.

Lunar and solar eclipses are bookends that mark beginnings and endings. The internal and external work we do in between can be powerful. Eclipse energy represents cycles that support you in aligning more deeply with your bigger goals in life and support you in breaking free from habits and patterns that keep you from growing and expanding.

To learn more about the transits and how they affect your personal Human Design chart and your energy, visit this website: freehumandesignchart.com

HOW TO USE THIS BOOK

The *2026 Quantum Human Design Evolution Guide* is a workbook with a weekly writing assignment, affirmation, and setup for Emotional Freedom Techniques (EFT). If you are not a fan of journaling, feel free to contemplate the prompts in whatever way works for you. You may walk with them, meditate on them, or even discuss them with your friends.

I am excited to share with you updated Quantum Human Design language. Over the years, it has become obvious to me that the vocabulary in Human Design is in need of an upgrade in response to evolutionary shifts and with respect to new research that shows how the language we use has the power to change your DNA. I hope you enjoy the new language!

Each of the Quantum Human Design gates and planets has a challenge associated with it. This is what you must triumph over to get the most out of the movement of the Sun, which occurs approximately every six days. Before you complete the writing assignment, read the challenge for each gate and contemplate what you need to do to get the most out of each of the weekly archetypes.

For the past few years, we've included the Earth transits to help you explore how you need to nurture and ground yourself each week. The short contemplation or exercise will help you use the energy of the Earth to stay aligned and supported so that you can better accomplish the themes highlighted by the Sun.

We've also added Mercury retrograde cycles. You'll learn about these key cosmic pauses that invite us to go inward and realign with our voice, our message, and our relationships.

The EFT is a powerful energy psychology tool that has been scientifically proven to change your emotional, mental, and genetic programming to help you express your highest potential. Each week you may work with a specific EFT setup phrase to help you clear any old energies you may be carrying related to the archetype of the week. (Learn more about how to use EFT here: quantumhumandesign.com/2026-guide)

You will also find exercises for each new moon, full moon, solar eclipse, and lunar eclipse complete with a writing/contemplation assignment and affirmation. You'll be guided in working with the theme of the lunar cycles and eclipses so that you can make the most of these powerful energy cycles.

Every Human Design year gives us a 365-day creative cycle that supports us in releasing what no longer serves us, allowing us to consciously increase our creative energy, grow, and evolve with the support of the stars.

May you have a prosperous and joyful 2026!

THE THEME OF THE YEAR
2026: THE YEAR OF CONSCIOUS CREATION

The year 2026 arrives like the first clear breath after a long and turbulent storm. For the past several years, the world has endured an unrelenting series of breakdowns—social, political, ecological, and spiritual. These outer disruptions have mirrored an internal dismantling, an unraveling of the stories, systems, and identities that once gave us a false sense of certainty. But in 2026, a subtle but profound shift begins to emerge. The outer planets—Saturn, Uranus, Neptune, and Pluto—have all changed signs, signaling not just a new chapter but the beginning of an entirely new epoch in human evolution.

These planetary movements are no small matter. The last time Uranus changed signs was in 2018; for Neptune, it was 2011; for Pluto, it was 2008; and for Saturn, 2023. By the time we enter 2026, all four of these heavyweights have fully established themselves in new territory. Saturn, the great teacher and architect of time, has moved into Aries. Uranus, the planet that sparks revolutions, has moved into Gemini, tasking us with the job of healing our own inner polarization and the limits of binary thinking. Neptune, planet of dreams and transcendence, has left its long sojourn in Pisces and now resides in fiery Aries as well. And Pluto, the alchemist and transformer, has taken its seat in Aquarius, where it will remain until 2043. Together, these transits signify the completion of a deep purging process and the beginning of something entirely new.

In 2026, the disruptive energies these shifts heralded in 2023–2025 begin to settle. The tectonic plates beneath our lives, having shifted and cracked open, now find a new resting place. The energy of this year is one not of destruction but of direction. The rubble of the old world has fallen. What remains is the sacred responsibility to build something better. If the past few years have been about deconstruction, 2026 is about conscious creation. It's the moment when we stop waiting for change to happen and realize that we are the change agents we've been looking for.

It is, quite literally, a year of hope and new beginnings.

But this isn't hope built on wishful thinking or bypassing reality. It is a grounded, embodied, and earned hope. With Saturn in Aries, we are called to take radical personal responsibility for our lives and the world we live in. Saturn here is not a distant authority figure. It's the voice within each of us that says, "No one is coming to save you. But you were never helpless to begin with." Aries is the sign of the pioneer, the spark of initiative, the place where fire meets form. Saturn's presence here asks us to take the seed of inspiration and do the daily, disciplined work of making it real.

Neptune in Aries adds another layer. After years of drifting in Pisces's oceanic dreamscape, Neptune in Aries ignites the visionary with the flame of action. This is not about vague spiritual aspirations or passive idealism. Now, the dream must become flesh. Now, the mystic picks up the sword—not to fight but to cut through illusion. Neptune in Aries reminds us that our spiritual calling is not separate from our worldly lives. It demands embodiment. Action. Courage. We are being invited to step fully into our purpose and bring it to life in practical, even radical, ways.

Meanwhile, Pluto in Aquarius ensures that our personal transformation is matched by collective evolution. Pluto is the slowest-moving planet and represents deep, often unconscious change. Its entrance into Aquarius signals a twenty-year revolution in how we relate to technology, power, and each other. While the initial years of Pluto's ingress into Aquarius have been marked by digital unrest, cultural polarization, and structural tension, 2026 marks a turning point. The breakdown has occurred. Now begins the rebuilding.

Even with this more harmonious energy emerging, the work is far from over. There is still chaos in the outer world. Institutions are still in flux. The climate crisis, economic instability, and social fragmentation continue to challenge us. But 2026 is different because we are different. We are no longer reacting from survival. We are no longer tangled in the pain and trauma of the past. The healing has taken place. The cords have been cut. The inner narrative has shifted.

2026 is the year we claim our title as conscious creators.

This means reprogramming our minds, our bodies, and our energy systems to focus forward. It means recognizing that intention isn't just a passive desire—it is a vibrational blueprint. Our thoughts, emotions, and actions are not isolated events. They are the building blocks of the future. With Jupiter transitioning from sensitive Cancer into radiant Leo in late 2026, we're given permission to shine again—to step into our creative power and lead with heart.

Jupiter in Cancer for most of the year nourishes the roots. It calls us to reconnect with family, ancestry, and the emotional intelligence that sustains community. It brings softness and safety where there has been hardness and fear. But when it moves into Leo, the energy turns outward. We are no longer holding the torch. We are lighting the stage. It's time to be seen, to lead, to celebrate what we're creating—not just in solitude, but in solidarity.

The astrological geometry of 2026 supports this shift. For the first time in years, the outer planets form a series of harmonious aspects—trines and sextiles—that suggest ease, support, and alignment. Where there were once blocks, there are now pathways. Where there was once resistance, there is flow. It's not about ease without effort—it's about effort that works. We are no longer trying to swim upstream. The current is with us—if we choose to direct it consciously.

And that's the key: consciousness. 2026 is not about returning to "normal." It's about refusing to return to the unconscious patterns that created so much of our collective pain in the first place. It's about standing on new ground—spiritually, psychologically, and energetically—and planting our flag. Saying, "This is who I am. This is what I stand for. This is the world I will help build."

In a very real way, the untangling process is complete. The veil has been lifted. The wounds have been acknowledged. The patterns have been named. We are no longer victims of our stories—we are authors. And the blank page of the future is waiting.

So, what comes next?

That is up to us. Not the politicians. Not the algorithms. Not the authorities. Us. In 2026, the invitation is to go beyond survival and into soul-level intention. To not just heal, but to create. To not just rebuild, but to reimagine. The planetary weather supports us in this endeavor. But, as always in astrology, the planets don't do the work for us—they simply mirror the energetic possibilities available.

This is our moment to step in, to step up, and to step out into the world as creators of the new era. An era that honors wholeness, justice, harmony, and joy. An era rooted in the wisdom of the past, the vision of the future, and the power of the present.

Welcome to 2026. The storm has passed. The soil is fertile. The future is calling.

It's time to build.

THE NODES

The Nodes represent the plot outline in the story of the year ahead. The nodal pairs reflect how we mature and evolve over the days ahead and what challenges we must overcome in order to fulfill the potential of this year.

Evolution is never linear. It's more like learning to ride a bike with training wheels. Just as we start with the training wheels close to the ground and raise them up until eventually we remove them as the rider gets more comfortable with stabilizing the bike, so does evolution require us to practice, learn new patterns, regulate our mindset, and then integrate new ways of being into our bodies as we grow.

This process of titrating our evolution is the theme of this year. We might feel wobbly, needing rest and time for practice and integration as we navigate our way forward. The Nodes give us a code for what we need to do to optimize our growth.

The first half of 2026 brings us into a powerful threshold of transition. From January through May, we are deeply engaged in the process of untangling ourselves from the past—ancestral patterns, inherited expectations, and internalized limitations that no longer reflect who we are becoming. It's a season of reckoning, where clarity arrives through release. We're shedding old roles and agreements we may not have consciously chosen, making space to reclaim our power and redefine our identity on our own terms. This is the necessary unraveling before a new weave can begin.

As we move closer to mid-May, a shift begins to take shape. Where the early part of the year was focused on clearing and letting go, a new energy begins to emerge—one that reveals glimpses of what's possible. The future doesn't arrive all at once, but we start to feel its quiet pull. This is a time to listen carefully to what's stirring inside, to notice what ideas or dreams keep returning, and to begin anchoring ourselves in trust. The question isn't just what we need to do next—it's what we need to believe in, what we're being asked to place our faith in, even before the proof arrives.

By July, the atmosphere becomes more intense and expansive. The inner fire that's been smoldering begins to burn brighter. There is momentum, but it comes with a call for deep trust and emotional resilience. We are invited to stretch our capacity—not just to act, but to believe more fiercely in what we cannot yet see. This season can feel passionate, even inflammatory at times, as old coping mechanisms and outdated structures continue to dissolve. But alongside that intensity is a growing strength. We're learning to hold the heat, to stay present in the transformation without needing to rush toward certainty.

Late summer into fall brings a period of refinement. The visions that have been emerging now ask to be tended with devotion. We are clarifying what truly matters, and this clarity sharpens our sense of purpose. The urgency to stay in alignment becomes undeniable. There is less tolerance for the ways we've compromised or diluted ourselves in the past. Now, our choices must reflect our deepest truth. We are not being asked to have it all figured out—but we are being asked to be honest, to be brave, and to stay grounded as we embody a new rhythm of living.

By the end of November, we enter the season of revolution. After a year of shedding, listening, and trusting, we arrive at a threshold of claiming. This is a time for bold clarity—a time to say what we stand for, what we are no longer willing to carry, and what must be dismantled in order for something new to rise. The line between old and new is no longer blurred. We're called to make definitive choices, not from fear or reactivity, but from a place of deep truth and devotion. The revolution is both personal and collective. It asks us to walk forward unburdened, aligned, and ready to cocreate the future with power, purpose, and unwavering faith.

January 1–May 14

South Node—Gate 40: The Gate of Restoration

North Node—Gate 37: The Gate of Peace

The South Node, aligned with the theme of retreat and renewal, is calling us inward. This energy asks us to slow down, to take space, and to honor the necessity of solitude—not as isolation, but as restoration. In a world that often equates movement with progress, this can feel deeply uncomfortable. The shadow expression of this node can leave us feeling lonely, disconnected, and unmoored. But this is not disconnection as punishment—it is disconnection as preparation. When we allow ourselves the grace of personal retreat, we replenish the vital energy we need to engage in life with clarity, integrity, and strength. This is especially important as we navigate new agreements and renegotiate the terms of our relationships, both personal and collective.

The North Node in Gate 37, the Gate of Peace, guides us toward a future where peace and equitability become the bedrock of human connection. This energy teaches us that we cannot cocreate, commune, or compromise when we are running on empty. The task here is to come to the table full—to pour into relationship, family, community, and justice from a place of wholeness. Gate 37 isn't just about peace for peace's sake—it's about building lasting harmony that honors both individual worth and collective well-being. It challenges us to renegotiate our relational contracts with an awareness of our emotional and energetic capacity and to ensure our agreements reflect mutual care, dignity, and value.

This transit is especially powerful because it activates both the Will Center and the Emotional Solar Plexus, touching the deepest themes of value, desire, and emotional integrity. These centers hold the memory of our ancestral karma—generational bargains and patterns rooted in survival, sacrifice, and scarcity. The planetary work now is to untangle ourselves from these outdated agreements so we can step into a new paradigm rooted in self-worth and mutual respect. We are not just healing ourselves; we are participating in the redefinition of value on a collective scale. This is the soul of social justice: to know the worth of all beings and to build systems that reflect that knowing.

In its shadow, this nodal axis may tempt us to regress—to cling to the comfort of the past, to restore old contracts and cultural agreements that no longer serve us. It may stir conflict where old bargains are broken or power imbalances are revealed. But harmony is not passive. The invitation here is not to avoid discomfort but to face it with courage. True peace is forged through action, not appeasement. We are being asked to heal the fracture between our inner depletion and our outer obligations, to restore ourselves first—so that when we rise, we do so ready to create a world built on just, sustainable, and soulful agreements.

May 14–July 25

South Node—Gate 59: The Gate of Sustainability

North Node—Gate 55: The Gate of Faith

As we navigate this cycle, we are being asked to cultivate a deeper relationship with faith—not as a passive belief, but as an active, generative force. Faith, in its truest expression, is the capacity to trust in the invisible blueprint, to believe in what has not yet taken form. It is the creative tension that holds space between vision and manifestation. Without faith, the architecture of the new cannot be completed. The scaffolding collapses under the weight of doubt. But with faith, every unseen piece finds its place. We become builders of possibility, guided not by what is, but by what can be.

Yet, faith cannot be sustained without the foundational belief in enoughness. To believe in a future, we must first believe in ourselves. We must feel, in our bones, that we are enough, that we have enough, and that we will receive enough. This is not wishful thinking—it is an energetic alignment with sufficiency. When we do not know what enough feels like, when we are ruled by scarcity or narratives of unworthiness, our ability to trust the process falters. We panic. We grasp. We retreat. The soul of faith withers in the presence of internal lack.

Gate 59, the Gate of Sustainability, brings this conversation into the body. It asks us to confront the stories and inherited beliefs that cause us to doubt our own sufficiency—doubts about our ability to give, to receive, to connect, to endure. This gate teaches that sustainability—whether in relationships, resources, or revolutions—requires inner clarity about what is enough. If we cannot see the enoughness in ourselves and each other, then faith becomes hollow, and creation becomes extraction. We lose the pulse of the future before it ever begins to beat.

This is the deeper invitation of this nodal season: to dismantle old perspectives that convince us we are lacking and to replace them with a sacred knowing that we are resourced, that life is resourced, that the Universe is reciprocal. Only then can we truly tap into the kind of faith that builds new worlds. The blueprint is waiting, but it can only be read by those who trust in their own sufficiency. Revolution, after all, is not just a fight—it is a reorientation to the truth of what is possible when we believe that we are enough.

July 25–November 24

South Node—Gate 29: The Gate of Devotion

North Node—Gate 30: The Gate of Passion

During this season, the South Node is gently drawing us back to the inner sanctum of devotion. It reminds us that faith isn't something we simply possess—it's something we cultivate. Faith must be built, tended, and practiced. Like a muscle, it grows stronger with use, especially when we consciously engage with it in times of uncertainty. We don't need faith when the path is clear; we need it when we are wandering in the dark with only a spark of vision to guide us. The invitation here is to create a consistent practice—a rhythm of remembering, trusting, and staying aligned even when evidence hasn't yet arrived. Devotion, then, becomes the scaffolding for faith. It gives shape and structure to our inner belief and anchors us in the unseen promise of what's to come.

As we turn toward the North Node, the evolutionary pull urges us to hold and tend the fire of vision. This is not the flickering light of a momentary impulse but the enduring flame that must be stoked with intentionality. The dream we're called to bring forth cannot be rushed. It must simmer. This is the energy of Gate 30—emotional intensity that, when properly directed, sustains the vision through time. Paired with Pluto's ongoing transit through Gate 41, the Gate of Imagination, we are given a potent alchemical formula: Imagination plus sustained emotional commitment equals manifestation. But if we remove the fire too soon or rush the process, we serve an undercooked dream, something not yet ready to nourish us or the world.

This pairing of nodal energies teaches us discernment and endurance. It asks us to be mindful of what we commit to. It is not enough to be passionate; we must be passionately aligned. We must know what is worth giving our energy to and be willing to sustain that commitment over time. If we misdirect our energy—if we say yes to the wrong things or burn with passion without purpose—then our fire becomes destructive instead of creative. It flares up and burns out. It leaves us empty instead of fulfilled. The deeper wisdom here is to choose what is truly worthy of our devotion and to let that devotion fuel a slow, steady transformation.

Ultimately, this cycle is about learning the difference between reaction and response, between short-term passion and long-term purpose. It is a call to step into mature faith—the kind of faith that keeps the fire alive even when results are slow to emerge. It is a time to tend our inner hearth, to be discerning with our emotional energy, and to say a holy yes only to what will truly sustain us in the becoming.

November 24–April 7, 2027
South Node—Gate 4: The Gate of Possibility
North Node—Gate 49: The Gate of the Catalyst

As we enter this final nodal chapter of the year, the narrative reaches a climactic turning point. There is a collective pressure—urgent and visceral—to determine what's next. We are seeking clarity, scanning the horizon for solid answers that will guide our next step. But instead of a tidy roadmap, we find ourselves in a liminal space of experimentation and exploration. This is a moment to test, to try, to stretch the boundaries of what we think is possible. Only through this active experimentation can we begin to establish new rhythms—sustainable, repeatable patterns that will serve as the foundation for the systems and structures of the future.

However, before construction begins, deconstruction is required. This nodal theme carries with it the necessity of release—of making space. It is not enough to tweak the old ways or simply reframe outdated beliefs; we are called to catalyze lasting change by cutting ourselves free from what no longer serves. This is the definitive separation from outdated values, a final turning point that demands our full commitment to the new. The opportunity here is nothing short of revolutionary: a revolution that reshapes our relationships, our communities, our agreements, and even the laws and social contracts that hold our world together.

Yet, this revolution must be intentional. The same energy that can liberate us can also tear us apart if misused. If we react from a place of wounded ego or unchecked emotion—if we rage against perceived injustice without anchoring ourselves in vision—we risk destroying the very things that are still worth preserving. The potential for reactivity is high, especially when emotions run hot, and the danger lies in mistaking impulsive rebellion for true evolution. This is a time for clear intention, for conscious action, for discernment between what must fall and what must endure.

Ultimately, the success of this cycle depends on our ability to unify rather than fracture, to hold the tension between destruction and creation with wisdom. The revolution we are capable of birthing now is one rooted in values that reflect compassion, clarity, and conscious design. This is our opportunity to step forward not with the bitterness of reaction, but with the power of deliberate reformation—one that honors the lessons of the past while anchoring firmly in the possibility of a more aligned future.

URANUS, NEPTUNE, AND PLUTO—
THE OUTER PLANETS AND GLOBAL THEMES

The outer planets—Jupiter, Saturn, Uranus, Neptune, and Pluto—are creating quite the evolutionary matrix for massive change. They have been setting the stage for quantum leaps in human evolution since 2024 and will continue to do so until early 2027.

We are moving into an era where individuality matters, and our world is structured in such a way that individuality is not obliterated or negated by the needs of the collective. At the same time, we will also feel obligated (in a good way) to our communities, each one of us playing our unique, vital, and irreplaceable role. The aggregate effort of individuals will keep us going, and we will all understand that we only rise when we all rise together. This is the dawning of the Quantum Era and the emergence of the Quantum Human, an evolution I discuss in my aptly titled book.

In 2026, we enter a defining moment in our human evolutionary journey as the outer planets—Uranus, Neptune, and Pluto—settle into their new astrological positions, along with Saturn and Jupiter, who join them in activating a fresh energetic climate. These planets, often called the "collective planets," shape not only personal growth but the very arc of our societal evolution. Where the inner planets stir day-to-day awareness, these giants move more slowly, setting the tone for long cycles of transformation. Each planet serves a distinct evolutionary function: Saturn tests our structure and discipline, Jupiter expands and blesses what it touches, Uranus shakes us loose from stagnation, Neptune opens us to the mystical realms of purpose and spirit, and Pluto dismantles old power structures to initiate deep, regenerative growth. Together, they are the architects of the mythic narrative we are all living through—especially now, as we begin to integrate the enormous energetic shifts of the last eighteen months.

URANUS

November 5, 2025 - Gate 8: The Gate of Fulfillment

April 28, 2026 - Gate 20: The Gate of Patience

Uranus, now stabilizing its transit through Gemini, serves as the evolutionary spark, disrupting what no longer works, catalyzing awakening, and urging innovation. Uranus doesn't ask for permission. It jolts us awake, pushing us to break with outdated paradigms, often through unexpected events or sudden insights. In Gemini, this Uranian current infuses our collective consciousness with revolutionary ideas, new technologies, and radical shifts in communication and learning. But revolutions aren't instant; they require repetition, trial, and recalibration.

When we harness this energy wisely—aligned with right timing and deliberate experimentation—we build something sustainable. But if we leap too soon, without learning the rhythm of change, we risk rebellion over revolution—chaotic fires rather than regenerative ones.

NEPTUNE

February 10, 2025 - Gate 25: The Gate of Spirit

May 23, 2026 - Gate 17: The Gate of Anticipation

August 23, 2026 - Gate 25: The Gate of Spirit

Neptune, the planet of spirit and higher consciousness, guides our inner alignment and reminds us of our cosmic contract. In 2026, Neptune moves between Gate 25, the Gate of Spirit, and Gate 17, the Gate of Anticipation. These transits invite us to embody our higher purpose with humility, devotion, and surrender. Gate 25 teaches us that our lives are not solely our own. We are expressions of a larger divine intelligence, and our purpose is not self-authored, but self-discovered through alignment. When Neptune moves to Gate 17, we begin imagining what's next—a vision shaped not by ego but by clarity of spiritual purpose. As it returns to Gate 25 in late summer, it reminds us again to keep the ego in service to the soul. Neptune's message is clear: To fulfill our potential, we must live as stewards of the Divine—not just creators, but cocreators.

PLUTO

January 30, 2025–February 24, 2028 - Gate 41: The Gate of Imagination

Pluto, the planet of death and rebirth, is the slow-burning fire behind the biggest transformations. Now positioned in Gate 41, the Gate of Imagination—the very starting point of the Human Design year—Pluto is initiating an entirely new chapter of the human story. This is not just a seasonal shift but a generational portal. Gate 41 is the seed gate. It births the spark of a dream, a vision, a possibility. Pluto's work is not gentle. It demands that we release the past, clear karmic residue, and surrender to the gravity of evolution. And yet, this Plutonic initiation is not without promise—it holds the potential for profound regeneration. Everything begins in the imagination. What we imagine now sets the trajectory for the future.

SATURN AND JUPITER

We finish up our overview of the major planetary movements by taking a closer look at Saturn and Jupiter. These two planets dance together in the sky, revealing the relationship between the work we must do and the rewards available to us when we do the work.

In the midst of these outer planet transits, Jupiter and Saturn also add important texture. By mid-2026, both will be situated in either fire or air signs—an unusual and potent configuration. Fire ignites, inspires, and burns through stagnation. Air disperses, communicates, and lifts consciousness. Together, they bring a season of explosive growth—mental, spiritual, and societal. When held with discipline and care, these elements create advancement, progress, and profound learning. But fire, if mismanaged, can burn indiscriminately. We are being asked to become skilled stewards of our creative power, to consciously wield fire as a force of clarity and constructive transformation.

Over the course of the year, the following gates are highlighted:

Jupiter

September 18, 2025–January 6, 2026 - Gate 62: The Gate of Preparation

January 6, 2026–March 6, 2026 - Gate 53: The Gate of Starting

March 6, 2026–March 16, 2026 - Gate 39: The Gate of Recalibration

March 16, 2026–May 13, 2026 - Gate 53: The Gate of Starting

May 13, 2026–June 13, 2026 - Gate 62: The Gate of Preparation

June 13, 2026–July 10, 2026 - Gate 56: The Gate of Expansion

July 10, 2026–August 4, 2026 - Gate 31: The Gate of the Leader

August 4, 2026–August 30, 2026 - Gate 33: The Gate of Retelling

August 30, 2026–September 27, 2026 - Gate 7: The Gate of Collaboration

September 27, 2026–November 2, 2026 - Gate 4: The Gate of Possibility

November 2, 2026–January 23, 2027 - Gate 29: The Gate of Devotion

Saturn

September 25, 2025–January 28, 2026 - Gate 36: The Gate of Exploration

January 28, 2026–March 19, 2026 - Gate 25: The Gate of Spirit

March 19, 2026–May 4, 2026 - Gate 17: The Gate of Anticipation

May 4, 2026–October 29, 2026 - Gate 21: The Gate of Self-Regulation

October 29, 2026–January 22, 2027 - Gate 17: The Gate of Anticipation

In 2026, the relationship between Saturn and Jupiter invites us into a profound refinement of both our inner and outer lives. Saturn, often considered the teacher or the expert builder, is calling us to root more deeply into our higher purpose and to trust in the unseen architecture of spirit. It asks us to become conscious stewards of the energy we are cultivating and transmitting, urging us to transcend outdated patterns and stories that limit our expansion. This isn't about bypassing reality with spiritual platitudes—it's about structuring our lives in a way that nurtures and aligns with the emotional frequency required for true evolution. Saturn wants us to hold steady, even in the face of uncertainty, and to stop outsourcing our authority to the realm of opinion and reaction. Instead, we are being asked to nurture the ego—not to diminish it but to train it as a faithful servant to our higher self, building sustainable foundations that allow us to embody our value and channel our energy with intention.

Jupiter, dancing in partnership with Saturn, brings the promise of expansion—but not expansion for its own sake. Rather, Jupiter is guiding us to grow in a way that is rooted, intentional, and sovereign. Before we leap into action or growth, we must return to the core of who we are and connect with what is true for us at the deepest level. This is not a time for superficial growth or ambition born of comparison or fear. It is a time to calibrate our energy to the new possibilities emerging on the horizon and to embody a practice of calling in miracles—not through force or hustle, but through authentic alignment. Jupiter supports us in rewriting the narrative of who we believe we are and what we believe we're capable of, encouraging us to lead not from power over others but from the power that comes from being fully rooted in truth.

Together, Saturn and Jupiter in 2026 create a kind of sacred tension—a push and pull between discipline and expansion, between contraction and trust. The shadow of this dynamic asks us to pay attention: Saturn warns us not to leap forward prematurely without cultivating the internal scaffolding required to hold what we're calling in. The structures we create on the outside must reflect the integrity we've developed on the inside. If we bypass this internal work, we risk building castles on sand. Jupiter, on the other hand, asks us to be mindful of the stories we tell ourselves when we feel afraid, to not overextend or attempt to recreate the past simply because the future feels uncertain. This is a year to resist the urge to go back and, instead, to ground our faith in a future that is still unfolding.

Ultimately, this powerful pairing is about maturity and magic. Saturn teaches us how to manage time, to build rhythms and practices that anchor us. Jupiter teaches us how to expand time—how to move beyond limitation and into the spaciousness of possibility. If we are willing to do the deep, sometimes uncomfortable, inner work Saturn demands of us, Jupiter will meet us with nourishment, abundance, and joy—not as a reward but as a natural outcome of alignment. Together, they ask us to remember that our lives are the soil from which the new world is seeded—and that the most powerful structures we can build are those designed to house the full expression of the truth of who we are becoming.

This year we must remember that even though fire can be destructive, in the cold of winter, fire warms and nourishes. It lights the way. It cooks the food and hardens the tools we use to build. Fire in its optimal state is a sacred tool—transformative, clarifying, and life-giving. When emotional, fire is out of control and driven by ego, fear, or rebellion. It can become wild and uncontrolled. The lesson of this season is to become wise fire-keepers—to tend the inner flame of purpose, clarity, and faith with care and reverence, knowing when to burn and when to stoke.

As we move through 2026, the retrogrades and directional shifts of these planets will serve as spiritual titrations. The back-and-forth rhythm is not regression but refinement. These oscillations help us metabolize change at a pace we can sustain. Retrogrades allow us to reflect, reevaluate, and recalibrate. They give us the space to close the door on what no longer serves while preparing the soil for what is to come. This in-between space is sacred. It is the womb of creation.

Ultimately, this entire astrological cycle is a profound invitation, a call to imagine and initiate a new world. The combined messages from Pluto, Neptune, and Uranus—along with Saturn and Jupiter and the Nodes—ask us to embody deeper integrity, cultivate spiritual clarity, and courageously innovate. We are being positioned not just to survive the storm, but to learn how to wield the elements with wisdom. This is the beginning of a new story—not written by fate but coauthored by each of us as we remember who we truly are and what we came here to create.

2026 ECLIPSE SEASON

Eclipses serve as celestial checkpoints. An eclipse is a high-octane celestial event that helps illuminate our karmic path, but just as these cosmic events can be visually striking, eclipses can also be a bit dramatic. Astrologically speaking, they speed up time. They open new doors by slamming others shut, so we often find abrupt and sudden shifts occurring during eclipses.

Though the shifts can be jarring, they can help us by speeding up the inevitable. So, if you've been dragging your feet, an eclipse will be sure to give you that extra push (or shove) needed to take action. While the results can be shocking, remember that these celestial events simply expedite the inevitable. These events were going to happen eventually.

Understanding transits helps you consciously harness the power of the transit and use it to your advantage. This knowledge won't necessarily help you avoid the intensity of these catalytic celestial events, but it will help you influence the outcome and better regulate your response. Remember, you can't always control what happens in your life, but you always have control over what you do with these events.

During solar eclipses, the Moon is directly between the Earth and Sun, so the Sun and the Moon are said to be in conjunction. For some time, the tiny Moon has the capability to block out the giant Sun and turn off the lights on Earth. This might take away our perspectives in life. Solar eclipses take away fixed patterns and push us into unknown realms. Though this might cause upheavals in our lives, solar eclipses are excellent growth promoters and powerful catalysts.

A lunar eclipse is an astronomical event that occurs when the Moon moves into the Earth's shadow, causing the Moon to be darkened. Astrologically, a lunar eclipse intensifies what needs to be brought to light in order for us to release, heal, align, or let go of limits that block us from fulfilling our goals and dreams. This energy delivers a powerful opening to growth by helping us explore what needs to be seen and revealed for us to create with greater integrity.

This year we work primarily with eclipses on the Virgo-Pisces and Leo-Aquarius axes.

The Leo-Aquarius eclipse axis invites us into a powerful evolutionary cycle that challenges the balance between personal identity and collective progress. Leo brings the spotlight to the self, urging us to own our voice, shine with authenticity, and courageously lead from the heart. It calls us inward to remember our inherent value and unique creative potential, asking, Who are you when you're fully expressed? Aquarius, its counterpart, shifts the focus outward—toward innovation, social change, and visionary community. It compels us to see beyond our individuality and take part in shaping systems that serve the greater good. This axis reminds us that our individual radiance isn't self-indulgent—it's essential for creating a future that honors the full diversity and brilliance of humanity.

As eclipses move through this axis, they bring moments of both inner reckoning and outer revolution. We are pushed to confront the parts of ourselves that still seek validation, recognition, or belonging and instead root our leadership in inner alignment and soulful truth. These eclipses often initiate quantum leaps in consciousness: They reveal outdated narratives, catalyze shifts in how we contribute to collective change, and spark new paradigms of leadership that are rooted in collaboration, authenticity, and shared vision. The Leo-Aquarius axis ultimately teaches us that inner work and self-expression are not separate from social transformation—they are the seeds of it.

The Virgo-Pisces eclipse axis draws us into a sacred dance between structure and surrender, where the tangible meets the mystical. Virgo invites us to refine, heal, and serve through grounded, practical action, bringing attention to the systems that support our well-being, our daily rituals, and our commitment to purposeful work. This is the axis of healing in motion, asking us to discern what is truly in service to our highest self and others. Pisces, in contrast, opens the portal to the unseen, enhancing our intuition, emotional sensitivity, and spiritual awareness. It softens the edges of logic and invites compassion, reminding us that healing is not only physical but also emotional, energetic, and deeply soul-based.

When eclipses occur on the Virgo-Pisces axis, they awaken both the inner healer and the mystic. We may be called to release the illusion of control, perfectionism, or overanalysis (Virgo's shadow) in order to deepen our trust in life's greater unfolding (Pisces's wisdom). These eclipses challenge us to bring spiritual insight into embodied practice—to ground our dreams in reality and let service be an act of devotion, not just duty. This axis supports the integration of emotional intelligence, energetic sensitivity, and holistic health, guiding us toward a life of aligned service where intuition and integrity walk hand in hand.

Below is a list of all the eclipse dates in this eclipse cycle, including the Human Design gates highlighted with each eclipse:

February 17, 2026 - Annular solar eclipse in Aquarius
Gate 30: The Gate of Passion

March 3, 2026 - Total lunar eclipse in Virgo
Gate 64: The Gate of Divine Transference

August 12, 2026 - Total solar eclipse in Leo
Gate 4: The Gate of Possibility

August 28, 2026 - Partial lunar eclipse in Pisces
Gate 55: The Gate of Faith

You will find special eclipse contemplations in this guide inserted on the dates of the 2026 eclipse events.

MY CHART

Using this information and your own chart, which you can get at freehumandesignchart.com, have fun coloring in your defined gates and centers on the chart below.

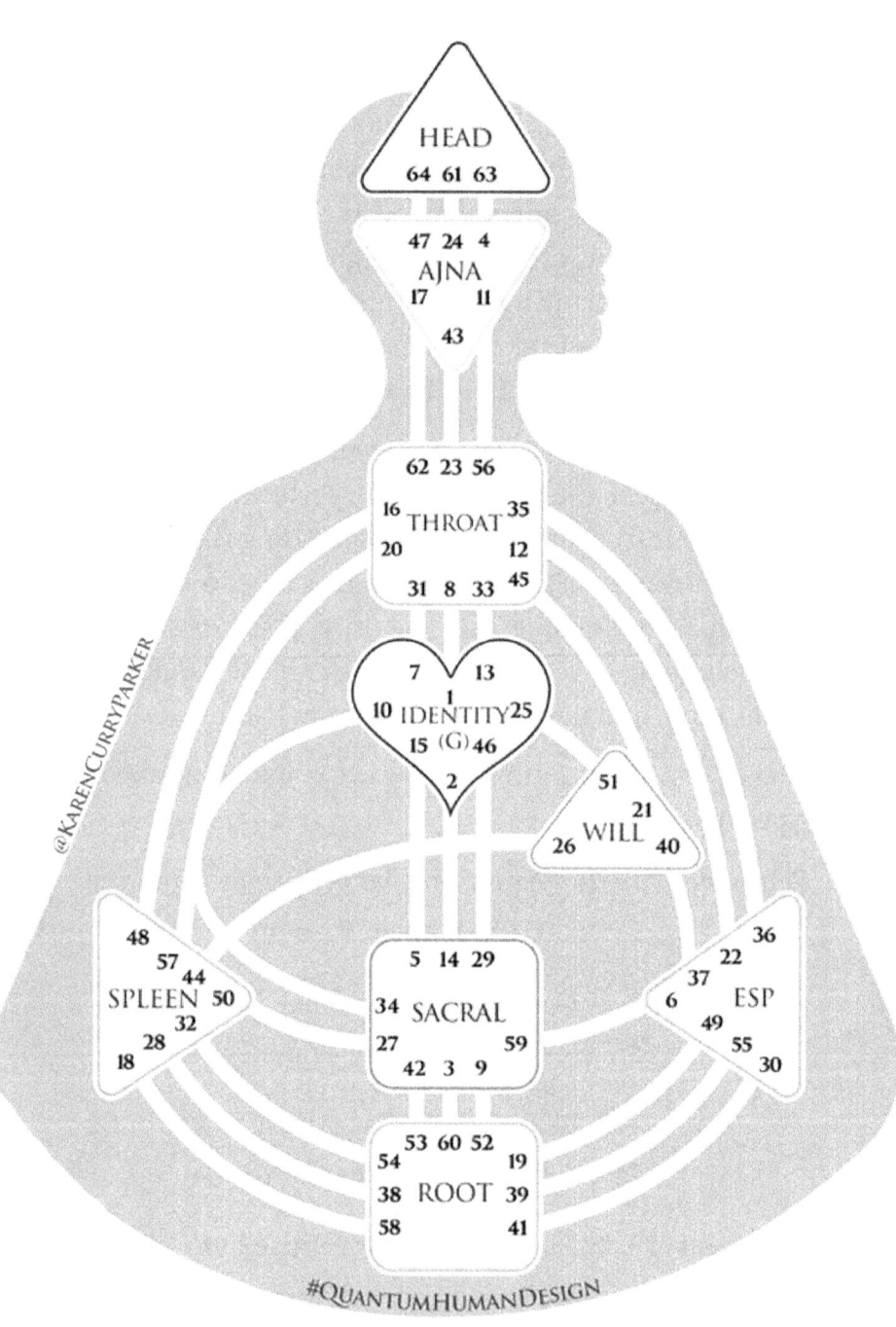

My Chart Highlights

My Type _____

My Profile _____

My Defined Centers _____

My Open Centers _____

My Conscious Sun _____

My Unconscious Sun _____

My Conscious Earth _____

My Unconscious Earth _____

QUANTUM HUMAN DESIGN CHART KEYNOTES

UNBALANCED EXPRESSIONS / OPTIMAL EXPRESSIONS OF TYPES

Traditional HD	Quantum HD	Unbalanced Expression	Optimal Expression
Manifestor	Initiator	Powerlessness Power struggles	Deeply connected to divine inspiration and the flow of Spirit Committed to the value of the role that only an Initiator can play To own their own power, know when to inform, and move forward when the timing is right To serve as a creative muse and a transformational agent of change
Generator	Alchemist	Quitting through frustration Trying to figure out what's next	To explore through responding, enduring, sustaining, practice, repetition, and correction to learn who they are and how they respond to life To cultivate a deep and aligned relationship to their purpose and path and to trust that the next level will be revealed when they are ready
Manifesting Generator	Time Bender	Quitting through frustration Anger Disruption	Aware of their power and speed Deeply conscious of those around them who will be impacted by their fast response to life Tuned in to their Sacral Center to wait to respond Alignment gives creative flow that brings change, transformation, and creativity Ability to act transforms people's perceptions of what is possible
Projector	Orchestrator	Feeling unheard and unseen Burnout	To nurture and care for their mind, body, and spirit with great deliberation To understand that timing and waiting work in their favor by resting between activations to restore their energy To know their value and to share with the right people at the right time To trust right timing Here to manage, guide, and delegate to conserve their energy
Reflector	Calibrator	Trying to fix others Feeling exhausted and disappointed with the world	Aware of their surroundings and the experience of their surroundings within them To feel in alignment with their community, like they are at home with the people and the environment around them To take the time to be in alignment with what is right for them A reflection that simply needs to be noticed and witnessed without the need for correction or fixing

QUANTUM HUMAN DESIGN CHART KEYNOTES

UNBALANCED EXPRESSIONS / OPTIMAL EXPRESSIONS OF LINES

TRADITIONAL HD	QUANTUM HD	UNBALANCED EXPRESSION	OPTIMAL EXPRESSION
1: Investigator	Resource	Fear of not knowing enough Fear of the unknown	To lay the information foundation for the security and safety of all of us To value and trust their curiosity To celebrate and value the depth of their knowledge
2: Hermit	Responder	Fear of disappearing and being isolated	To integrate knowledge, energy, and wisdom, and wait for the readiness of others to call them out To need alone time to rest, integrate, and regenerate to be ready when it's time to share what they know
3: Martyr	Explorer	Fear of failure	To explore and experience possibilities and to share their experiences with others to protect and serve them To need to experiment and try things to gain proficiency and share insights with others
4: Opportunist	Stabilizer	Fear of loss or being in limbo	To lay the foundation of community and connection and prepare the way for sharing and spreading of ideas To learn how to facilitate change, be in the flow, and use this knowledge to help others To bring stability to the community with their wisdom
5: Heretic	Visionary Leader	Fear of not being truly seen or heard Subject to false expectations of others	To serve as a karmic mirror for others and to support the healing process through their reflection by teaching and sharing the highest potential of humanity possible Able to gauge who they are here to lead; to teach, lead, and inspire those who are ready
6: Role Model	Adept	Fear of failing their life purpose	To experience, integrate, and demonstrate the highest potential of consciousness on the planet and to quietly show us how to live it Phase 1: To fearlessly experiment and explore to discover what works best Phase 2: To integrate what they've learned and rest, heal, learn, and explore their own creative plane Phase 3: To live as the ruler of aligned and authentic living—to show the world by walking their talk

QUANTUM HUMAN DESIGN CHART KEYNOTES

UNBALANCED EXPRESSIONS / OPTIMAL EXPRESSIONS OF CENTERS (DEFINED AND OPEN)

Traditional HD	Quantum HD	Unbalanced Expression	Optimal Expression
Head (Defined)	Quantum Interface	Feeling uninspired	A conduit for inspiration To use inspiration with responsibility and awareness To recognize their role as an inspirational force in the world
Head (Open)		Confusion Pressure Self-doubt Feeling lost	The observer of inspiration To trust that the inspirations that are theirs to follow will reveal themselves on the material plane
Ajna (Defined)	Divine Translator	Closed-minded Locked in negative thought patterns	To generate expansive ideas and concepts and envision them until the details of how to materialize these ideas reveal themselves
Ajna (Open)		Under pressure to figure things out Fear of the unknown Trying to hold a fixed vision	To see ideas from different perspectives and be open-minded about how they envision and imagine To embrace unlimited possibilities and make peace with the unknown
Throat (Defined)	Activation	Speaking without waiting for right timing Using words irresponsibly	To wait for the right cues and clues to know how to share information or words that elevate and increase potential
Throat (Open)		Feeling pressure to speak Trying to prove their value Not waiting for right timing or right people	To trust the divine flow of information To trust that when the timing and the environment is correct, they'll be able to share what they know with words that best meet the needs of others
Identity (G-Center) (Defined)	Calibration	Afraid they won't be loved for expressing their authentic self	To recognize that they are designed to love, to be empowered, to control their own personal narrative, to use their life in service to their higher self, to stay vital, to explore how much goodness they're willing to allow, and to share it compassionately with the world To trust that when they express their authentic self, they are moving in a direction that supports their sustainability and abundance and energetically shows the way to others

Traditional HD	Quantum HD	Unbalanced Expression	Optimal Expression
Identity (G-Center) (Open)		Questioning their lovability Struggling with direction	Deeply wise about the potential of the story of humanity To choose which elements of the human condition and narrative they want to integrate as part of themselves To know that who they are is evolving and expanding To use other people's narratives to consciously calibrate their own direction
Will (Defined)	Resource	Pushing and using force of will Low self-worth Avoiding and depleting self Burnout	To give from abundant resources and stay consistently resourced to avoid cycles of depletion and exhaustion To live and create from a place of knowing their value and taking right actions to take up their right place and right space To live and create in physical, resource, identity, moral, and energetic integrity To use conscious rest and re-Sourcing themselves as a way of sustaining integrity To know that who they are has a unique and vital role in serving others
Will (Open)		Taking actions and choice to prove their value to others	To evaluate integrity and alignment with value in others To gauge their level of investment in circumstances that do not match their own value and values To have the freedom to consciously choose what they consider to be valuable and build their life around it To live from an internal sense of their own value To learn to trust in sufficiency To fully embody enoughness ("I *am* enough…")
Emotional Solar Plexus (Defined)	Creative	Making emotional decisions in the moment Feeling disappointment, anger, frustration, or bitterness	To know how to deliberately envision an outcome and wait to ensure the desire for the outcome stays consistent no matter how their mood fluctuates
Emotional Solar Plexus (Open)		Giving up what they need to be happy Compromising on their dreams or values for others	To hold their emotional frequency even when others struggle to sustain theirs
Sacral (Defined)	Evolution	Pushing too hard Compromising on their inner wisdom Quitting before they self-actualize	To trust their inner alignment and innate responding nature to allow the unfolding of life's intelligent plan of action through them

Traditional HD	Quantum HD	Unbalanced Expression	Optimal Expression
Sacral (Open)		Not knowing when enough is enough Burning out by overdoing it	To experience life-force energy and vitality and to use it to guide and direct others to do the work To know what needs to be done and tap into resources to facilitate getting it done without actually having to do it themselves
Spleen (Defined)	Self-Actualization	Hypervigilant Avoidance or overpreparing Driven by fear of not getting things done	The presence and awareness to know what they need to know when they need to know it and do what they need to do when they need to do it to be aligned with sustainability, integrity, and expansion
Spleen (Open)		Holding onto things, people, or situations longer than is healthy Preparing for the worst case	To use alignment with courage to uplift others To overcome fear, find presence, and be centered
Root (Defined)	Divine Timing	Not waiting for right timing Burnout Not being ready when the time aligns	Deeply connected to the energy flow state that is experienced when the timing for action is aligned
Root (Open)		Feeling pressured or stressed Not trusting right timing Burnout	To use adrenaline energy in a sustainable way to ensure right action at the right time

QUANTUM HUMAN DESIGN CHART KEYNOTES

UNBALANCED EXPRESSIONS / OPTIMAL EXPRESSIONS OF CIRCUITS AND SUBCIRCUITS

TRADITIONAL HD	QUANTUM HD	UNBALANCED EXPRESSION	OPTIMAL EXPRESSION
Individual	Transformation	Rebelling in reaction to feeling uncertain and insecure Ignoring right timing and readiness and sharing what they know without waiting Feeling hurt, left out, and the need to compromise who they are to feel loved and accepted Not honoring the transformation they bring enough to value themselves and their unique contribution to the world	The ability to stay true to their authentic identity, with the awareness that they are fulfilling the full expression of their identity and inspiration, to create a wave of new possibility for humanity To serve as a global change agent by simply being the fullest expression of themselves To know that their authentic story transforms the world
Individual Integration	Transformation Unifying	Reactive Depleted from pushing against right timing and failing to fulfill potential due to a lack of self-love and self-trust	The ability to be responsively powerful in alignment with inner and outer timing and love while serving the fulfillment of the full potential of the human condition
Individual Centering	Transformation **Calibration** (aura-busting)	Impulsively following their own path without respect to how it impacts others Taking actions that overcompensate for feeling unlovable Low self-worth Disconnection from purpose and heart and a distrust of Source/God	The ability to embody a deep relationship and trust of Source, higher self, and the fulfillment of purpose to lead others by demonstrating the way To initiate others into following their own hearts by showing the world what it looks like to live from the heart
Individual Knowing	Transformation Gnostic	Sharing what they know before people are ready Feeling outcast, strange, or alienated because people aren't ready for what they know Exhausting themselves by pushing their knowingness at the wrong time or with the wrong people	The ability to trust in what they know that they know and to trust that they'll know what they need to know when they need to know it The ability to trust in their purpose as a transformational agent on the planet and to let timing and circumstances inform them about when they need to share what they know To sow the seeds of change with their knowledge and transform the way people think, create, and connect to Source

Tribal	Sustainability	Fear of not having enough, creating hoarding, hiding, stealing, and war	The ability to create sustainable resources and share them with others
		Refusal to share out of fear of lack	The deep understanding of sharing and the embodiment of love as a verb
		Selfish actions or martyrdom	
		Depletion, exhaustion, and burnout that creates tension and projection	The ability to create peaceful agreements that are rooted in the possibility of win-win negotiation and justice
		Compromising what they really want for the sake of others and feeling resentful and exhausted	The management of resources that allows them to share what they have from a place of sufficiency
		Failure to take care of themselves so that they have more to give	The ability to respond to the needs of others in a sustainable, peaceful, and just way
Tribal Defense	Sustainability Nurture (aura-busting)	Codependency	The ability to do the work necessary to nurture and sustain resources
		Overcaring	
		Assuming responsibility for things they're not responsible for and making impulsive, defensive choices that can lead to war and destruction	To educate for the sake of cultivating the right values that are rooted in nurturing, sustainable choices
			To build the foundation of love in action
Tribal Ego	Sustainability Economic	Letting fear and lack create overwhelm and misuse of power and resources	The ability to respond to the right need at the right time to create sustainable value and shared resources
Collective	Synergy	Rigidly adhering to old patterns or unproven ideas and trying to construct false systems with inaccurate information	The ability to understand past experiences and patterns and to use these understandings to build collective infrastructures and systems that allow us to fully express our humanity and to ensure the survival of the species
		Rigidly adhering to old systems and stories that are not supported by truth	
Collective Logic/ Understanding	Synergy Pattern	Adhering so rigidly to patterns that they miss the pattern interrupt	The ability to test and experiment with information in order to understand patterns
		Letting fear, doubt, and suspicion keep them from changing the pattern	The use of patterns to predict future outcomes
		Discounting the wisdom of the heart	
Collective Sensing	Synergy Miracle	Allowing ungrounded fantasy and old painful experiences from the past to set the tone and the direction for life	The ability to use the power of storytelling and personal narrative to break old patterns and to expand the story of what is possible
		Chaos or rigidity	

QUANTUM HUMAN DESIGN CHART KEYNOTES

UNBALANCED EXPRESSIONS / OPTIMAL EXPRESSIONS OF THE GATES

Gate	Traditional HD	Quantum HD	Unbalanced Expression	Optimal Expression
1	Self-Expression	Purpose	An erratic or purposeless life Panic Anxiety due to a feeling of "failing" at a life mission Pressure to create something unique in the world Struggle to find purpose Hiding out because the purpose feels too big, too much, or egotistical	The ability to know the authentic self and a deep connection with a life purpose
2	Keeper of the Keys	Allowing	Experiencing stress and fear Ultimately compromising on what they want and who they are because they don't trust that they're supported Valiantly self-sufficient to the point of burning themselves out Never asking for help	To set intentions and move solidly toward the fulfillment of the authentic self with complete trust that they are supported in being the full expression of who they are and their life purpose, even if they don't know how or what the support will look like To trust in Source To live in a state of gratitude
3	Ordering	Innovation	Feeling pressured and panicked to share an idea or innovation Burning themselves out trying to override divine timing	The ability to embrace and integrate new ideas and new ways of doing things To appreciate their unique way of thinking and being and to trust that as an innovator on the leading edge of consciousness, their time to transmit what they're here to bring forth will come, so they wait and cultivate their ideas with patience
4	Answers	Possibility	Self-doubt and fear that they have an idea that they can't figure out The pressure to try to share or implement the idea before it has had time to seed the manifestation Acting too soon without waiting for the right timing	The ability to experience an idea as a possibility, to use the idea as a seed for the imagination, and to use the imagination to create an emotional response which then calibrates the heart and attracts experiences and opportunities that match the possibility into their life
5	Patterns	Consistency	Life seeming like a constant struggle to stay connected and live habitually in a way that creates stability, sustainability, and a fulfilled expression	The ability to stay consistent with habits and choices that bring them closer to living true to who they are through alignment and not overusing willpower

6	Friction	Impact	Feeling desperate, emotionally reactive, lacking, and invisible Willing to do whatever it takes to take resources and energy for their own good, regardless of the means Fearing that they'll never be seen or heard	To maintain a high frequency of emotional energy that supports equitability, sustainability, and peace To use their emotional alignment to influence others and to serve as an energetic beacon of peace and sufficiency
7	Self in Interaction	Collaboration	Struggling and fighting to be seen and recognized as the leader at cost to their energy and the fulfillment of their purpose	To embrace that power comes from supporting, influencing, and collaborating with leadership To recognize that they don't have to be the figurehead to influence the direction that leadership assumes—the chief of staff is often more powerful than the president The energy to unify people around an idea that influences the direction of leadership
8	Contribution	Fulfillment	Feeling panicked and disconnected from their life purpose Thinking that their life purpose is something they have to do versus someone they have to be Trying to be someone they're not in an attempt to serve as a role model	To push the edges and boundaries of authentic self-expression and realize that being the full expression of their authentic self *is* their life purpose To use their authentic expression to inspire others to fulfill themselves
9	Focus	Convergence	Feeling pressured to figure out where to place their focus Overwhelmed and confused by too many options and choices Unable to see the relationship between ideas and actions and missing the important details	The ability to see the big picture and prioritize where to focus their energy
10	Love of Self	Self-Love	Questioning their lovability Struggling to prove their love-worthiness Giving up and settling for less than what they deserve and blaming others for their circumstances and situations Victim consciousness	To see their love for themselves as the source of their true creative power
11	Ideas	The Conceptualist	Desperately trying to force every idea they have into manifestation	The awareness that they are a vessel for ideas To understand that those ideas are for them to hold and protect until the right person comes along to share them with To relax as the vessel and know that not all ideas are theirs to build upon To use the power of their inspiration to

				stimulate the imagination of themselves and others
12	Caution	The Channel	Struggling to try to speak ideas into form when it's not the right time Letting hesitancy and caution freeze them Trying to force ideas and words	To know that their voice is an expression of transformation and a vehicle for divine insight The words they speak and the insights and creativity they share have the power to change others and the world When articulate, they know people are ready to receive their wisdom If they struggle to find the words, they have the courage to wait until it feels more aligned
13	The Listener	Narrative	Staying stuck in old stories Holding on to old past pains Staying the victim in a story that repeats itself because their personal narrative is stuck	The ability to use the power of personal narrative to create with power and intention
14	Power Skills	Creation	Fearing and worrying about money Willing to compromise their right work to do whatever they have to do for material gain	The ability to be at peace about having resources In a constant state of trust that everything they need will show up in their outer reality in accordance with their alignment with Source To use their resources to increase the resources for others To no longer work for material gain and instead to work for the sake of transforming the world and being in the flow of life To know that support flows from alignment with their heart
15	Extremes	Compassion	Self-judgment and extreme habits that are frenetic and nonproductive Trying to force their natural waves of rhythm into the daily practices and habits that society defines as successful and struggling with follow-through Denying their own heart Being too afraid to do what feels right	The ability to trust their own flow and rhythm, to trust that they will have cycles that disrupt old patterns and force them to recreate their direction and flow To set parameters for their creativity, work within the parameters when it feels right, and rest in between because nature has rhythm and extremes To change old rhythms and patterns to align them with greater compassion
16	Skills	Zest	Having a pattern of leaping into the unknown without sufficient preparation Not assessing whether an idea or inspiration is actually an	The courage to trust their own intuition that the timing is right and that they are ready enough, even if they don't know exactly how their journey will unfold To keep faith in the outcome

			expression of understanding Leaping without looking Holding themselves back when they know the time is right because others tell them they're not ready	
17	Opinions	Anticipation	Sharing opinions that degrade options Embracing opinions as truth and acting on them Creating personal and collective narratives that are negative and filled with doubt	To use the power of their mind to explore potentials and possibilities that stretch our ideas about what else is possible in the human condition To use their thoughts to inspire others to think bigger and bolder To use their words to inspire and set the stage for creating energy that expands potential
18	Correction	Re-Alignment	Being critical Sharing criticism without respect for the impact More concerned with their own "rightness" than assessing whether their insight is actually adding to more joy in the world	To see a pattern that needs correcting and wait for the right timing and circumstances to correct and align it To serve joy
19	Wanting	Attunement	Being overly sensitive and shutting down or compromising their own needs and wants Feeling disconnected from others as a way of coping with being overly sensitive Being emotionally clingy or needy as a way of forcing their natural desire for intimacy	The ability to sense the emotional needs of others and their community and to know how to bring the emotional energy back into alignment with sufficiency and sustainability The ability to be emotionally vulnerable and present to increase heart-to-heart connections
20	Metamorphosis	Patience	Acting before the time is right Failing to listen to their inner guidance and to prepare Feeling pressure to take action before the time is right and feeling frustrated or quitting	The ability to trust their intuition, to know what needs to be set in place, what people need to be gathered, and what skills need to be grasped, and to be ready when the time is right To trust in the right timing and heed the intuition to get ready
21	The Treasurer	Self-Regulation	Feeling the need to control life, others, resources, etc., out of fear that they aren't worthy of being supported	The ability to regulate their inner and outer environment to sustain a vibrational frequency that reflects their true value The ability to be self-generous and to set boundaries that maintain their value and support them in being sustainable in the world To take the actions necessary to honor their unique role in the cosmic plan

22	Openness	Surrender	Fearing that they are not supported Holding back or stifling their passion because they think they can't afford to pursue it Compromising, settling, or letting despair regulate their emotional energy, causing the creative process to feel shut down or stuck	The grace to know that they are fully supported by the universal flow of abundance and to pursue their passion and their unique contribution to the world no matter what To trust that they will be given what they need when they need it in order to make their unique contribution to the world
23	Assimilation	Transmission	Needing to be right An anxiety or pressure to share what they know with people who aren't ready and then to feel despair or bitterness that others don't understand things the way that they do	The ability to translate transformative insights for people that offer them a way to change the way they think To share what they know with awareness of right timing and to trust their knowingness as an expression of their connection to Source
24	Rationalization	Blessings	Protecting themselves by staying stuck in old patterns Refusing to transform Allowing less than what they deserve	To recognize all experiences have the potential for growth and expansion To redefine the stories of their experiences to reflect what they learned and how they grew Grateful for all their life experiences and able to liberate themselves from stories that no longer serve them
25	Love of Spirit	Spirit	Fearing and mistrusting of Spirit Using their life strictly for personal gains regardless of the impact on others Ego in the lowest expression Not feeling worthy of being loved by Source and using their willpower to create instead of alignment	To connect with Source with consistency and diligence so as to fulfill their divine purpose, the true story of who they are, and the role they play in the cosmic plan To use their alignment with Source as a way of healing the world
26	The Trickster	Integrity	Struggling with remembering their preciousness and settling for less than what they want Letting unhealed past trauma keep them stuck in a limiting narrative Failing to trust in their support and compromising on their moral values Neglecting their self-care because they don't think they deserve it	To live in moral, energetic, identity, physical, and resource integrity with courage and trust To set clear boundaries and take the actions necessary to preserve the integrity of their right place

27	Responsibility	Accountability	Codependency Feeling guilty or making others feel guilty Overcaring Martyrdom	The ability to support, nurture, and lift others up To sense and act on what is necessary to increase the well-being of others and the world To feed people with healthy food and healthy nourishment to ensure that they thrive To hold others accountable for their own self-love and self-empowerment
28	Struggle	Adventure/ Challenge	Refusing to take action out of fear that the journey will be too painful, wrought with struggle, or that they will fail Feeling like a failure Falling into victim consciousness	To share from their personal experience, their struggles, and their triumphs To persevere and know that the adventures in their life deepen their ability to transform life into a meaningful journey To understand that their struggles help deepen the collective ideas about what is truly valuable and worthy of creating
29	Perseverance	Devotion	Overcommitting Not knowing when to let go and when enough is enough Failing to commit to the right thing Burning out and depleting themselves because they don't say yes to themselves Doing something just because they can, not because they want to	The ability to respond to committing to the right thing To know that their perseverance and determination changes the narrative of the world and shows people what is possible Their devotion sets the tone for the direction that life takes them
30	Desire	Passion	Burnout Impatience and not waiting for the right timing Misdirected passion that is perceived as too much intensity Leaping into chaos	The ability to sustain a dream, intention, and vision until they bring it into form To inspire others with the power of their dream To inspire passion in others
31	Democracy	The Leader	Pushing and seizing leadership for the sake of personal gain or being afraid to lead and not feel worthy of serving as a leader	The ability to be able to listen, learn, hear, and serve the people they lead and to assume and value their right leadership position as the voice for the people they are leading
32	Continuity	Endurance	Letting the fear of failure cause them to avoid preparing what they need to do Not being ready when the timing is right Pushing too hard, too fast, and too long against right timing	The awareness of what needs to be done to make a dream manifested reality The ability to set the stage, prepare, and be ready The patience and trust that once the stage is set, the timing will unfold as needed to serve the highest good of all To translate divine inspiration into readiness

33	Privacy	Retelling	Staying stuck and sharing a personal narrative rooted in pain, disempowerment, and victimhood	The ability to translate a personal experience into an empowering narrative that teaches and gives direction to others To find the power from the pain To wait for the right timing to transform or share a narrative so that it has the greatest impact on the heart of another
34	Power	Power	Being too busy to tune into the right timing and the right people Feeling frustrated with pushing and trying to make things happen Forcing manifestation with little results Depleting themselves because they're pushing too hard	The ability to respond to opportunities to unify the right people around a transformative and powerful idea when the timing and circumstances are correct
35	Change	Experience	Bored with life Letting the boredom of life cause them to settle for a life that never challenges the status quo	The ability to know which experiences are worthy and worthwhile To partake in the right experience and share their knowledge from the experience for the sake of changing the story of what's possible in the world
36	Crisis	Exploration	Not waiting for the right timing and leaping into new opportunities without waiting for alignment, causing chaos Leaping from opportunity to opportunity without waiting to see how the story will play out and never getting to experience the full fruition of the experience	The ability to hold a vision, sustain it with an aligned frequency of emotional energy, and bring the vision into form when the timing is right The ability to stretch the boundaries of the story of humanity by breaking patterns To create miracles through emotional alignment
37	Friendship	Peace	Desperately struggling to find peace outside of themselves Trying to control the outer world to create inner peace	The ability to stay connected to sustainable peace and to respond to life by generating peace no matter what is happening in their external reality To create the emotional alignment to make peaceful choices no matter what's going on in the outer world
38	The Fighter	The Visionary	Struggling for the sake of fighting Engaging in meaningless disputes Aggression and struggle	The ability to know what's worth committing to and fighting for To use their experiences to craft a vision that anchors the possibility of something truly meaningful and worthy in the world To serve the world as a visionary

#			Challenges	Gifts
39	Provocation	Recalibration	Feeling overwhelmed by lack and panicking	The ability to transform an experience into an opportunity to shift to greater abundance
			Hoarding or overshopping because of fear of lack	To see and experience internal or external lack and use their awareness of lack to recalibrate their energy toward sufficiency and abundance
			Provoking and challenging others and holding others responsible for their own inner alignment with sufficiency	
40	Loneliness	Restoration	Martyrdom	The ability to retreat as a way of replenishing their inner and outer resources and to bring their renewed self back into community when they are ready so that they have more to give
			Loneliness and blaming that causes them to compromise what they need and try to prove their value by overdoing and overgiving	
41	Fantasy	Imagination	Imagining worst-case scenarios and fixating on them	The ability to use their creative imagination to generate ideas about new abundant opportunities in the world
			Denying their creative capacity and abdicating their creative power	To sustain these abundant visions, share them when necessary, and use their imagination to break old patterns and limiting beliefs
			Being afraid to share other options because they defy the current expectations or patterns	Able to hold the vision of a miracle that transcends expectations
			Afraid of being judged by others for being a dreamer	
42	Finishing Things	Conclusion	Pressure, confusion, self-judgment for not being able to get things started	The ability to respond to being put into opportunities, experiences, and events that they have the wisdom to facilitate and complete
			Avoiding or putting off things that need to be completed, creating a backlog of projects that can lead to overwhelm	To know exactly what needs to be completed to create the space for something new
			Finishing things prematurely due to pressure	
43	Insight	Insight	Feeling despair or frustration related to having knowledge but struggling to share what they know	The ability to tap into new knowledge, understandings, and insights that expand people's understanding of the world
			Experiencing lightning bolts of knowingness and clarity but feeling overwhelmed by their inability to articulate what they understand	To align with the right timing and trust that they'll know how to share what they know when they need to share it
			Not waiting for the right time to share what they know and feeling alone with their wisdom	
44	Energy	Truth	Hesitating out of fear that the patterns of the past are insurmountable and doomed to	The ability to see patterns that have created pain
				To bring awareness to help themselves and

			repeat themselves	others break old patterns and transform pain into an increased sense of value and alignment with purpose
45	The King or Queen	Distribution	Diva energy Selfish leadership that is rooted in lack and showing off Holding back Overcompensating for a lack of self-worth with narcissism Fear of not being seen as a leader and reacting by being controlling, pompous and egotistical, or bombastic	The ability to understand that knowledge and material resources are powerful and to know how to use both as paths of service that sustain others and help others grow their own abundant foundation
46	Love of Body	Embodiment	Disconnected from the body Hating the body Avoiding nurturing or taking care of the body Avoiding the commitments and consistency necessary to fully embody life force Hiding or disfiguring the body	To recognize that the body is the vehicle for the soul and love the body as a vital element of the soul's expression in life To nurture, be grounded in, and fully care for the body To savor the physicality of the human experience To explore how to fully embody the spirit in their body and be committed to seeing how much life force they can embody into their physical form
47	Realization	Mindset	Quitting or giving up an inspiration because they can't figure out how to make it happen Feeling defeated and broken because they think they have ideas that they can't manifest	To engage in hopeful, inspired thoughts no matter what is going on around them To use inspiration as a catalyst for calibrating emotional frequency and the heart
48	Depth	Wisdom	Frozen in inadequacy Afraid to try something new or to go beyond their comfort zone because they think they don't know or that they're not ready	The wisdom to explore and learn the depth of knowledge necessary to create a strong foundation for action and proficiency The self-trust to have faith in their ability to know how to know and to trust their connection to Source as the true source for their knowledge
49	Principles	The Catalyst	Quitting too soon as a way of avoiding intimacy Compromising on their value and upholding agreements that no longer serve them Creating drama and fighting for outdated values that no longer serve the higher good	The ability to sense when it's time to hold to a value that supports their value The ability to inspire others to make expansive changes that embrace higher principles and a deeper alignment with peace and sustainability The willingness to align with a higher value

50	Values	Nurturing	Overcaring Letting guilt stop them from sustaining themselves Holding to rigid principles and struggling to allow others the consequences of their choices	The ability to nurture themselves so that they have more to give others The intuition to know what others need to bring them into greater alignment with love To commit to higher principles that sustain in the name of peace and love To teach and share what they have to increase the well-being of others
51	Shock	Initiation	Letting the shock of disruption cause them to lose connection with their true purpose and with Source Bitter or angry with God Trying to control life and depleting themselves from the energy necessary to hold themselves back	The ability to consciously use cycles of disruption and unexpected twists and turns of faith as catalysts that deepen their connection to Source and to their life and soul purpose
52	Stillness	Perspective	Attention deficit Letting overwhelm freeze them and cause them to fail to act Putting their energy and attention in the wrong place and spending their energy focused on something that bears no fruit	The ability to see the bigger perspective and purpose of what is going on around them and to know exactly where to focus their energy and attention to facilitate the unfolding of what's next
53	Starting Things	Starting	Reacting to the pressure to get an idea started Feeling like a failure because everything they start against right timing fails Afraid to start anything because of the trauma of their past "failures" Starting everything and never reaping the rewards of what they start	The ability to sit with inspiration and be attuned to what the inspiration wants and needs To launch the initiation sequence for an idea—and then let the idea follow its right course with trust in the flow
54	Drive	Divine Inspiration	Reacting to the pressure that they have to fulfill an inspiration and using force to push the inspiration into form—even though it might not be their idea or dream to manifest or the right time to bring it forth	The ability to cultivate a deep relationship with the divine muse To nurture the inspirational fruits of the muse and serve as a steward for an inspiration by aligning the idea energetically, laying foundational action, and building
55	Spirit	Faith	Indecisiveness Fear and lack Hoarding, keeping from others, fighting to take more than their share Not trusting Source and drawing on	The ability to hold the emotional frequency of energy and the vision for a creation To trust in sufficiency so deeply that they're able to create without limitation

			Will to create	
56	The Storyteller	Expansion	Getting lost or stuck in stories and narratives that are limiting Telling stories that contract and deplete the energy of others	The ability to share stories and inspirations that stimulate expansive and possibility-oriented thinking in others for the sake of stimulating powerful emotional energy that creates evolution and growth
57	Intuition	Instinct	Being so afraid of the future that they are stuck Not trusting themselves and their own instinct Knowing what needs to be done to prepare for the future and failing to act on it	The ability to sense when it is the right time to act To intuitively know what needs to be made ready to be prepared for the future and follow through on it
58	Joy	Joy	Denying joy Avoiding the practice of proficiency Feeling guilty or ashamed to do what they love	To harness the joy of proficiency and refine their practice until they reach fulfillment of their potential To live in the flow of joy
59	Sexuality	Sustainability	Feeling like they have to fight or struggle to survive Feeling the need to penetrate others and force their "rightness" on them Letting fear of lack cause them to craft relationships and agreements that are unsustainable	To trust in sufficiency and to know that when they create abundance, there is great fulfillment in sharing To craft partnerships and relationships that sustain them and the foundation of their lives
60	Acceptance	Conservation	Holding on and not allowing for growth Fighting for the old and rebuking change Letting the overwhelm of change and disruption create stagnation and resistance	The ability to find the blessings in transformation Optimism To know how to focus on what is working instead of what's not
61	Mystery	Wonder	Allowing the pressure to know why to create bitterness or victimhood that is often perpetuated in a rationalized pattern	The ability to see purpose in a bigger perspective that transcends the smaller details of an experience or event To stay in a state of innocence and confidence as a way of sustaining powerful creativity

62	Details	Preparation	Fear and worry Overpreparation Allowing their plan to override the flow	The ability to be attuned to what is necessary to be prepared and to trust that their alignment will inform them of everything that they need Relaxed by awareness that they'll know what they need to know when they need to know it
63	Doubt	Curiosity	Doubt (especially self-doubt) that leads to suspicion and the struggle for certainty The unwillingness to question an old idea The loss of curiosity	The ability to use questioning and curiosity as a way of stimulating dreams of new possibilities and potentials Thoughts that inspire the question of what needs to happen to make an idea a reality
64	Confusion	Divine Transference	Feeling pressure to try to manifest a big idea Feeling despairing, inadequate, or ungrounded if they don't know how to make an idea a reality Feeling deep mental pressure to figure out an idea Giving up dreaming	The ability to receive a big idea and to serve the idea by giving it their imagination and dreaming To trust that they'll know how to implement the idea if it is theirs to make manifest Ability to hold the energy of an idea for the world

EVOLUTION GUIDE

JANUARY 22, 2026

GATE 41: IMAGINATION

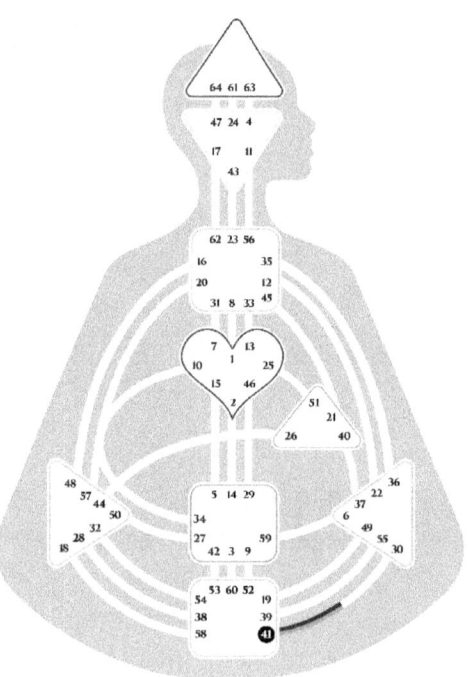

CHALLENGE:

To learn to use your imagination as a source of creative inspiration and manifestation. To experience the world and imagine more abundant possibilities. To stay connected to your creative fire.

AFFIRMATION:

I am a creative nexus of inspiration for the world. My ideas and imaginings inspire people to think beyond their limitations. My ideas stimulate new possibilities in the world. I am a powerful creator; my creative thoughts, ideas, and inspirations set the stage for miracles and possibilities that will change the story of humanity.

JOURNAL QUESTIONS:
- Do I own my creative power?
- How can I deepen my self-honoring of my creative power?

EFT SETUP:
Even though I am afraid my dreams won't come true, I deeply and completely love and accept myself.

EARTH:
GATE 31: LEADERSHIP

What is your place of service? Who do you serve? What can you do to feel more empowered and influential in your life?

JANUARY 28, 2026

GATE 19: ATTUNEMENT

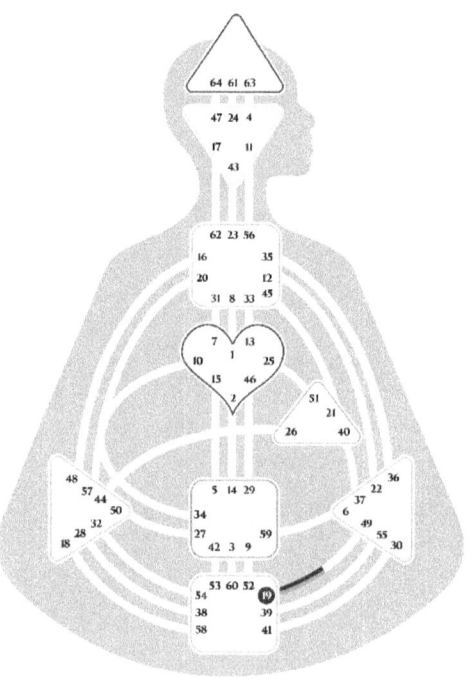

CHALLENGE:

To learn how to manage being a highly sensitive person and not let your sensitivity cause you to compromise what you want and who you are. To learn to keep your own resources in a sustainable state so that you have more to give. To not martyr yourself to the needs of others. To learn how to become emotionally intimate without being shut down or codependent.

AFFIRMATION:

I am deeply aware of the emotional needs and energy of others. My sensitivity and awareness give me insights that allow me to create intimacy and vulnerability in my relationships. I am aware and attuned to the emotional frequency around me, and I make adjustments to help support a high frequency of emotional alignment. I honor my own emotional needs as the foundation of what I share with others.

JOURNAL QUESTIONS:
- Am I emotionally present in my relationships?
- Do I need to become more attuned to my own emotional needs and ask for more of what I want and need?

EFT SETUP:
Even though it is scary to open my heart, I now choose to create space for deep intimacy and love in my life, and I deeply and completely love and accept myself.

EARTH:
Gate 33: Retelling

What personal narratives are you telling that might be keeping you stuck, feeling like a victim, or feeling unlovable? How can you rewrite these old stories?

FEBRUARY 1, 2026

FULL MOON

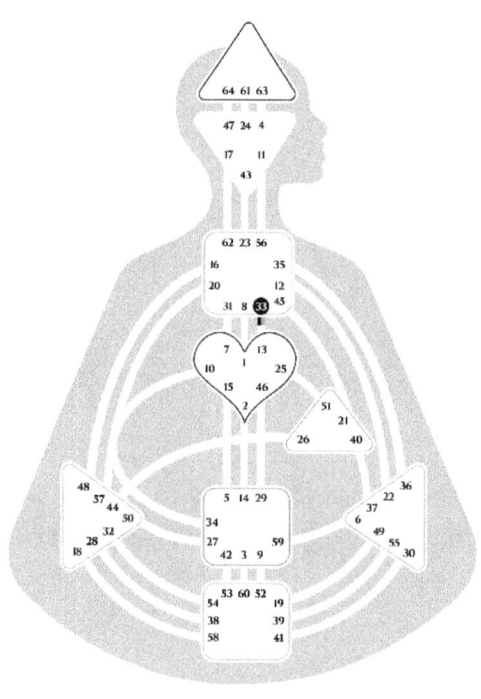

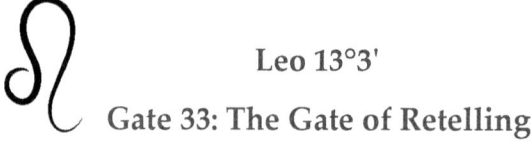

Leo 13°3'

Gate 33: The Gate of Retelling

Full moon energy invites us to explore what we need to release and let go of in order to stay in alignment with our intentions.

The full moon on February 1, 2026, brings with it an illuminating and catalytic energy—one that shines a bright, clarifying light on what is no longer aligned with our creative path. Full moons always invite release, but this one asks us to go deeper. It calls us to confront and shed the narratives, beliefs, and old stories that are silently directing our choices and influencing the trajectory of our lives. This moon is a mirror and a magnifier. It reveals what's ready to be rewritten so we can adjust our direction and reclaim the authorship of our personal myth with renewed clarity and purpose.

This particular lunar event activates Gate 33, the Gate of Retelling, placing the spotlight on the stories we carry, the stories we tell, and the stories we continue to live by—whether consciously or not. Gate 33 teaches us that our words, spoken and internalized, hold power. They are the architecture of identity. Under the light of this full moon, we are called to pause, reflect, and reclaim the sacred role of storyteller—not just as a way of processing the past but as a creative force that reshapes the future. The challenge here is to take full authorship over who we say we are, to narrate our lives from the seat of sovereignty rather than from unconscious repetition or inherited belief.

A key part of reclaiming that sovereignty is letting go of the narratives that cast us as victims. This isn't about denying what has happened or pretending pain didn't exist. It is about choosing not to let the pain define us. This is where forgiveness becomes alchemical. Forgiveness isn't about erasing the past—it's about releasing the emotional charge and the psychic weight that binds us to it. It's about liberating ourselves from the loop of retelling a disempowering story over and over again. When we forgive, we aren't saying that what happened was right— we are saying that we are more than what happened. We are reclaiming the power to choose how the story ends.

This full moon invites us into the sacred act of narrative transformation. It asks: What story are you ready to release? What version of yourself is waiting to be voiced? As we bless and release the chapters that have shaped us, we begin to create a new trajectory—not by force, but by resonance. This is the time to speak yourself into alignment. To take the raw materials of your experience and alchemize them into wisdom, compassion, and creative power. You are the narrator now. And with this full moon as your witness, you get to choose what comes next.

CHALLENGE:

The lesson of this full moon cycle is learning to reclaim authorship over your personal narrative by consciously releasing the stories that no longer serve your growth. It's an invitation to transform pain into power, to forgive without forgetting, and to align your words and identity with the truth of who you are becoming—not who you've been.

OPTIMAL EXPRESSION:

The optimal expression of this full moon energy is the radiant clarity that comes from owning your story with courage and compassion—speaking your truth not as a wound, but as wisdom. It's the empowered release of old narratives and the intentional choosing of a new creative direction that reflects your growth, sovereignty, and inner alignment.

UNBALANCED EXPRESSION:

In its unbalanced expression, this full moon may stir up unresolved emotions, causing old stories to resurface with the weight of blame, shame, or regret. Rather than serving as a catalyst for healing, the light of the Moon can amplify feelings of powerlessness if we remain attached to a narrative that centers on what was done to us rather than what we are now capable of choosing. This distortion can manifest as defensiveness, rumination, or the compulsive need to retell the same disempowering story in a loop, keeping us emotionally tethered to the past.

When we resist the invitation to forgive or redefine the story, we risk reinforcing an identity rooted in victimhood rather than agency. The shadow of Gate 33 can lead to silence born of suppression or storytelling that distorts rather than heals—either clinging to secrecy or wielding words as weapons. In this unbalanced state, the full moon's light feels harsh instead of illuminating, revealing truths we may not be ready to face. But even in its intensity, this energy is a call to realignment—reminding us that liberation begins the moment we decide to narrate our lives from the voice of our wisdom, not our wounds.

CONTEMPLATIONS:

- What stories am I still carrying that define me through the lens of what happened to me rather than what has awakened within me?
- Where am I giving my power away by keeping silent—or by telling a version of my story that doesn't reflect who I am becoming?
- What needs to be forgiven—not to condone the past, but to free myself from its emotional gravity?
- What creative direction or calling has been quietly waiting for me to release this old version of myself?
- If I were to rewrite my story today, what would I say about who I am and what I stand for?

AFFIRMATION:

I release the stories that no longer define me and reclaim my power as the author of my life. With clarity, courage, and compassion, I speak a new truth—one rooted in wisdom, sovereignty, and the creative force of who I am becoming.

FEBRUARY 2, 2026

GATE 13: NARRATIVE

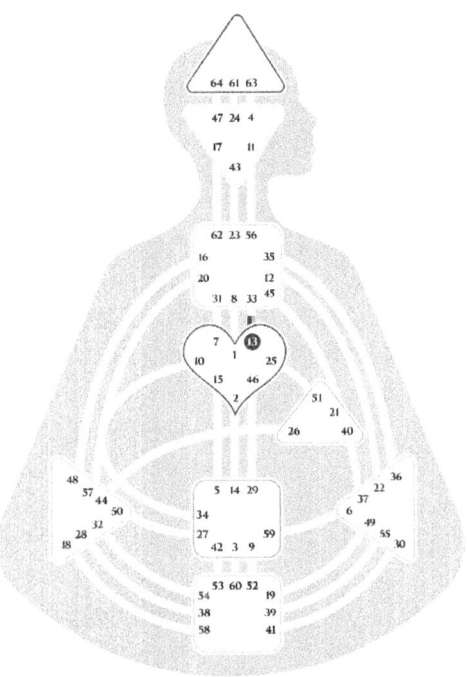

CHALLENGE:

To forgive the past and redefine who you are each and every day. To tell a personal narrative that is empowering, self-loving, and reflects your value and your authentic self. To bear witness to the pain and narrative of others and offer them a better story that allows them to expand on their abundance and blessings.

AFFIRMATION:

The story that I tell myself and the one I tell the world set the tone and direction for my life. I am the artist and creator of my story. I have the power to rewrite my story every day. The true story I tell from my heart allows me to serve my right place in the cosmic plan.

JOURNAL QUESTIONS:

- What stories about my life am I holding on to?
- Do these stories reflect who I really am and what I want to create in my life?
- What or who do I need to forgive in order to liberate myself to tell a new story?
- What secrets or stories am I holding for others? Do I need to release them?
- The true story of who I really am is…

EFT SETUP:

Even though I'm afraid to speak my truth, I now share the truth from my heart and trust that I am safe, and I deeply and completely love and accept myself.

EARTH:

Gate 7: Collaboration

Make a list of all the times when your influence has positively directed and impacted leadership and important ideas. Stay open to working in teams or groups. Find support and encouragement in collaboration with others this week.

FEBRUARY 8, 2026

GATE 49: THE CATALYST

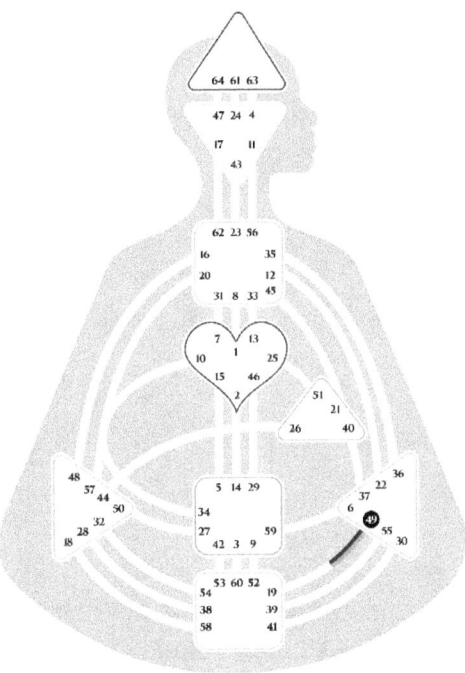

CHALLENGE:

To not quit prematurely, failing to start a necessary revolution in your life. To not hold on to unhealthy situations, relationships, or agreements that may compromise your value and worth.

AFFIRMATION:

I am a cosmic revolutionary. I am aligned with higher principles that support the evolution of humanity. I stand for peace, equity, and sustainability. I align with these principles, and I stand my ground. I do the work to create the intimacy necessary to share my values with others. I value myself and my work enough to only align with relationships that support my vital role.

JOURNAL QUESTIONS:

- Am I holding on too long? Is there a circumstance and condition that I am allowing because I am afraid of the emotional energy associated with change?
- Do I have a habit of quitting too soon? Do I fail to do the work associated with creating genuine intimacy?
- What do I need to let go of right now to create room for me to align with higher principles?

EFT SETUP:

Even though my emotional response causes me to react or freezes me, I deeply and completely love and accept myself.

EARTH:

Gate 4: Possibility

Take some time this week to contemplate new ideas and possibilities for your life. Dreaming and daydreaming support refining focus and alignment this week.

FEBRUARY 13, 2026

GATE 30: PASSION

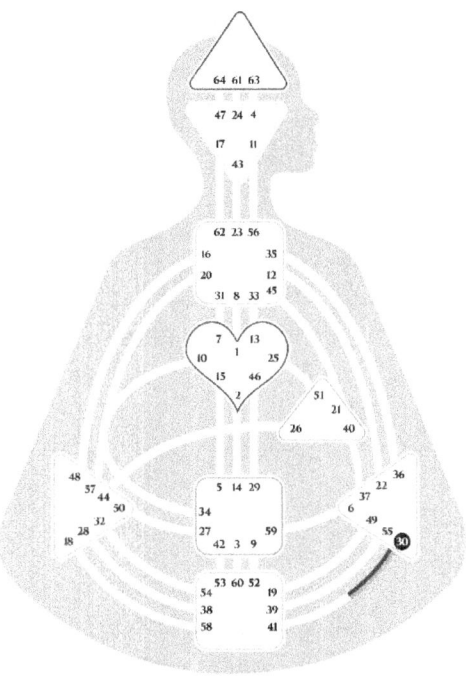

CHALLENGE:
To be able to sustain a dream or a vision without burning out. To know which dream to be passionate about. To not let passion overwhelm you and to wait for the right timing to share your passion with the world.

AFFIRMATION:
I am a passionate creator. I use the intensity of my passion to increase my emotional energy and sustain the power of my dream and what I imagine for life. I trust in the divine flow, and I wait for the right timing and the right circumstances to act on my dream.

JOURNAL QUESTIONS:

- What am I passionate about? Have I lost my passion?
- How is my energy? Am I physically burned out? Am I burned out on my idea?
- What do I need to do to sustain my vision or dream about what I am inspired to create in my life?
- Do I have a dream or vision I am avoiding because I'm afraid it won't come true?

EFT SETUP:

Even though my excitement feels like fear, I now choose to go forward with my passion on fire, fully trusting the infinite abundance of the Universe, and I deeply and completely love and accept myself.

EARTH:

Gate 29: Devotion

Who would you be and what would you choose if you gave yourself permission to say no more often? What would you like to say no to that you are saying yes to right now? What obligations do you need to take off your plate right now?

FEBRUARY 17, 2026

NEW MOON ANNULAR SOLAR ECLIPSE

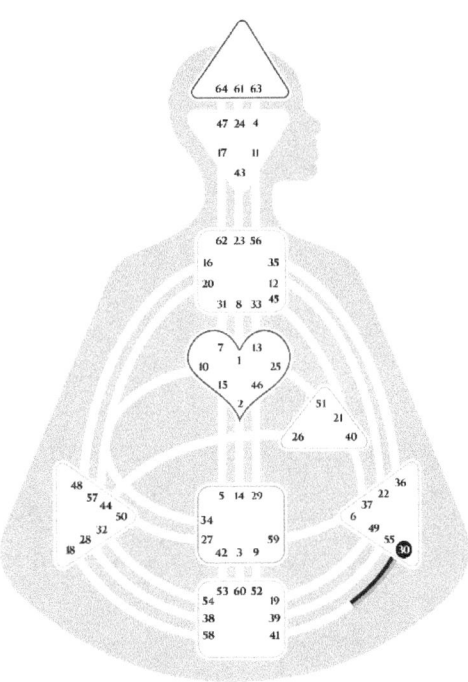

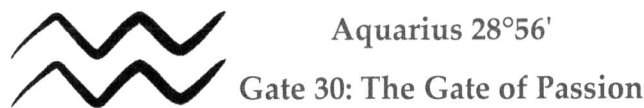

Aquarius 28°56'

Gate 30: The Gate of Passion

New moon energy invites us to explore how we can deepen our alignment with our intentions and asks us to focus on what we want to grow and expand on in our lives. Eclipse energy amplifies the intensity of the new moon. A solar eclipse signifies new beginnings.

The February 17, 2026, new moon arrives with potent force as an annular solar eclipse in Aquarius, activating deep themes of creative sovereignty and collective transformation. This eclipse continues the larger arc of evolution brought forward by the Leo-Aquarius eclipse axis, asking us to reconcile the tension between personal leadership and communal responsibility, between self-expression and social innovation. This lunation, opening a new emotional and creative cycle, invites us to reignite the spark of our inner fire—to clarify what we are truly passionate about and what legacy we are willing to devote our energy to creating.

In Quantum Human Design, this eclipse highlights Gate 30, the Gate of Passion—a deeply emotional energy that stirs the cauldron of longing, desire, and raw, human hunger to feel deeply alive. This is not a passive dream. This is the kind of yearning that insists on action, vision, and perseverance. It challenges us to ask: What am I passionately committed to? What fuels my vision—and how am I tending to that fire over time? The eclipse marks a portal of ignition but also one of responsibility: to build and sustain the energetic capacity required to hold the dream, nurture it, and see it through.

This is also a call to emotional maturity. Passion without regulation burns hot and fast—bright, but fleeting. The emotional wave of Gate 30 carries intensity and, in its shadow expression, can manifest as emotional reactivity, impulsive decision-making, or overwhelming craving without grounding. Without self-awareness and care, this energy can lead to burnout or discouragement, especially when the results don't match the urgency of our inner desire. We may feel tempted to force things before they're ready, pushing past the natural rhythms of right timing.

But when we meet this energy with grace, emotional regulation, and devotion to the long arc of becoming, it becomes a sacred fuel source. This eclipse invites us to become wise stewards of our emotional energy—learning to harness intensity without being consumed by it. It teaches us that passion is not just a spark; it is a fire that must be sustained, stoked, and respected. In doing so, we become aligned with the essence of true leadership: not domination or demand but the magnetic, sustained power of vision in motion.

As this eclipse resets the emotional template of your dreams, let it be a reminder that your passion is sacred—but only when nourished by patience, emotional clarity, and right timing does it have the power to become real. Let this moment be your invitation to recommit to what matters most and to practice the inner discipline required to carry your fire into the future.

CHALLENGE:

The major lesson of this eclipse is learning to channel emotional intensity into sustainable passion by regulating your inner fire rather than being ruled by it. To maximize growth, you must cultivate patience, emotional clarity, and trust in divine timing—honoring your vision without forcing its unfolding.

OPTIMAL EXPRESSION:

The optimal expression of this eclipse's energy invites you to connect deeply with what truly lights you up and to cultivate the emotional wisdom needed to sustain that passion over time. It's about pacing your fire—honoring your vision with care, devotion, and trust in right timing. When you allow your emotions to fuel aligned choices rather than reactive ones, you create space for lasting, meaningful action. In this state, your passion becomes a steady flame—one that not only inspires but also carries the power to shape your future with purpose and authenticity.

UNBALANCED EXPRESSION:

The unbalanced expression of this eclipse's energy may show up as emotional reactivity, urgency, or a desperate push to make something happen before it's truly ready. You might feel overwhelmed by the intensity of your desires, chasing passion without clarity or burning yourself out in pursuit of a vision that lacks grounded structure. When you're disconnected from your emotional rhythm, it's easy to mistake intensity for alignment and force outcomes rather than allowing them to unfold in right timing. In this state, passion becomes erratic or exhausting, leaving you feeling discouraged, depleted, or frustrated when things don't move as quickly as you hoped.

CONTEMPLATIONS:

- What am I truly passionate about right now—and how do I know it's aligned with my deeper purpose rather than a temporary emotional high?
- What practices or boundaries help me regulate my emotional energy so I can sustain my passion without burning out?
- Where in my life am I trying to force timing, and how can I surrender more fully to the natural rhythm of my creative process?
- What vision am I committed to nurturing over time, even when progress feels slow or uncertain?
- How can I transform emotional intensity into steady, inspired action that supports both my personal growth and the greater good?

AFFIRMATION:

I honor the fire of my passion with patience, trust, and devotion. I allow my emotions to guide—not drive—me as I nurture my vision in perfect timing.

FEBRUARY 19, 2026

GATE 55: FAITH

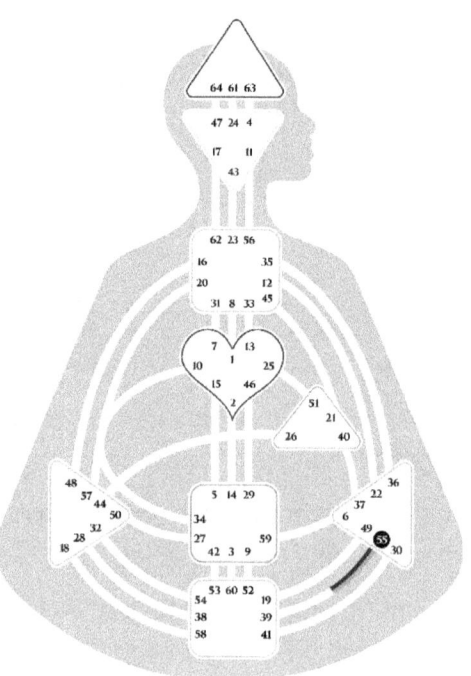

 **CHALLENGE:**

To learn to trust Source. To know that you are fully supported. To become proficient in the art of emotional alignment as your most creative power.

 **AFFIRMATION:**

I am perfectly and divinely supported. I know that all my needs and desires are being fulfilled. My trust in my support allows me to create beyond the limitation of what others think is possible, and my faith shows them the way. I use my emotional energy as the source of my creative power. My frequency of faith lifts others and opens up a greater world of potential and possibility.

JOURNAL QUESTIONS:
- Do I trust that I am fully supported? What do I need to do to deepen that trust?
- How can I align myself with abundant emotional energy? What practices or shifts do I need to make in my life to live and create in a more aligned way?
- Do I surround myself with beauty? How can I deepen my experience of beauty in my life?
- What do I have faith in now? What old gods of limitation do I need to stop worshipping?
- Go on a miracle hunt. Take stock of everything good that has happened in my life. How much magic have I been blessed with?

EFT SETUP:
Even though I struggle with faith and trusting Source, I deeply and completely love and accept myself.

EARTH:
Gate 59: Sustainability

Notice your energy this week. Are you feeling vital and sustainable? If not, what can you do to rest and renew yourself this week?

FEBRUARY 24, 2026

GATE 37: PEACE

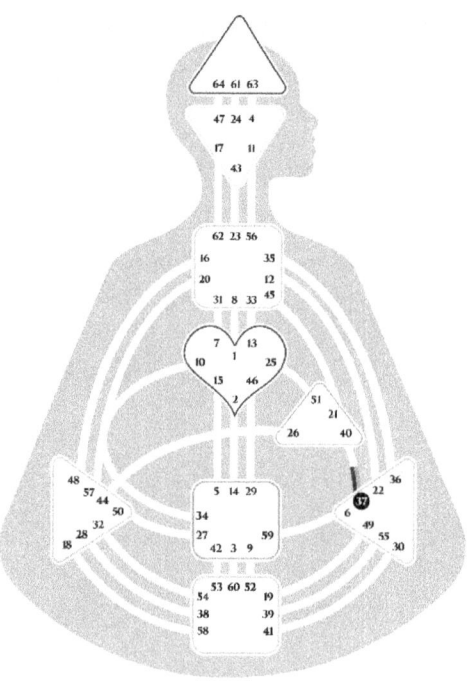

CHALLENGE:

To find inner peace as the true source to outer peace. To not let chaos and outer circumstances knock you off your center and disrupt your peace.

AFFIRMATION:

I am an agent of peace. My being, aligned with peace, creates an energy of contagious peace around me. I practice holding a peaceful frequency of energy, and I respond to the world with an intention of creating sustainable peace.

JOURNAL QUESTIONS:
- What habits, practices, and routines do I have that cultivate my inner alignment with sustainable peace?
- When I feel that my outer world is chaotic and disrupted, how do I cultivate inner peace?
- What do I need to do to cultivate a peaceful emotional frequency?

EFT SETUP:
Even though I struggle to create peace and harmony in my life, I deeply and completely love and accept myself.

EARTH:
Gate 40: Restoration

We are grounded in rest, renewal, and reconnecting to our purpose this week. Take some time to truly nourish your body, mind, and spirit so that you have a full tank of energy reserves for the days ahead.

FEBRUARY 26, 2026–MARCH 20, 2026

MERCURY RETROGRADE

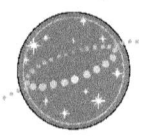

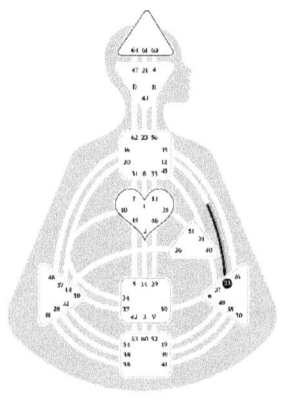
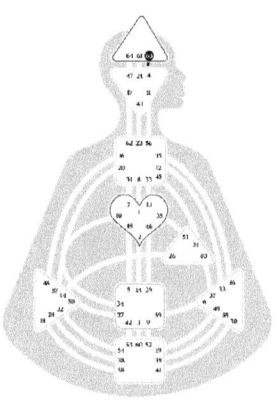
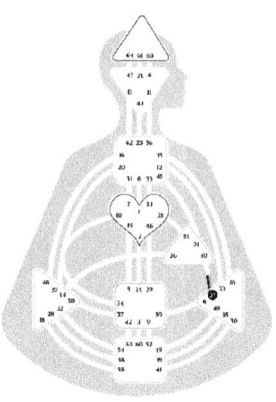

        Gate 22   Gate 63   Gate 37

The Gate of Surrender   **The Gate of Curiosity**   **The Gate of Peace**

Retrograde cycles encourage us to go inward to explore the themes the planets give us. Mercury is the planet associated with communication. When Mercury goes retrograde, it gives us an opportunity to go inward and contemplate how we can better align ourselves to have greater influence and impact in the world. Take your time to find the right words during this cycle. Do your best to not make big decisions, sign contracts, or make large purchases. Expect delays. Breathe and be patient with others (and yourself)!

This Mercury retrograde invites a profound inner journey—one that asks us to press pause on the need to force, to prove, or to control outcomes. As Mercury retraces its steps through Gate 22, the Gate of Surrender; Gate 63, the Gate of Curiosity; and Gate 37, the Gate of Peace, we're offered an opportunity to assess the foundations of our faith—both in ourselves and in the unfolding of life.

Gate 22 calls us to soften. It reminds us that grace and trust are not passive qualities but powerful stances of cocreation. True surrender is not about giving up; it's about letting go of the illusion that we are the sole architects of our future. Mercury's presence here encourages us to reflect: How much trust do we truly carry? How gracefully do we allow what we cannot yet control?

As Mercury moves into Gate 63, doubt may arise. Self-doubt, especially, can become a disruptive force during this cycle. Yet the lesson of Gate 63 is not to eliminate doubt but to use it as a portal to deeper inquiry. When we lose our curiosity, we lose our capacity to see possibilities.

This retrograde cycle challenges us to keep asking questions—not from fear, but from wonder. Can you stay open, even in uncertainty?

Finally, Mercury's retrograde path through Gate 37 reminds us that inner peace is not something we demand—it's something we cultivate. It arises when we align with our true values and stop fighting against the natural rhythms of life. Peace is the reward of surrender, the gift of trusting both the timing and the process of becoming.

The shadow of this retrograde lies in our impulse to fight, force, and fix. When we let doubt win, when we disconnect from the peace that comes from within, we try to muscle our way forward. But this retrograde whispers another way: Let go. Surrender the struggle. Stay curious. Return to inner harmony. Trust that what is yours will not miss you—and what is coming is already on its way.

CHALLENGE:

The core challenge of this Mercury retrograde cycle is learning to release the need to control outcomes and resist the pull of self-doubt. As Mercury moves through the Gates of Surrender, Curiosity, and Peace, we're asked to trust the unseen timing of life rather than force progress. The true test is not whether we can make something happen but whether we can stay open, curious, and connected to our inner peace even when clarity is elusive. Doubt—especially self-doubt—threatens to close us off from possibility, replacing trust with fear and curiosity with limitation. To overcome this challenge, we must soften, listen inward, and remember that alignment cannot be rushed—only received.

OPTIMAL EXPRESSION:

The optimal expression of this Mercury retrograde cycle is a deep return to trust—an embodied surrender that opens the door to grace, insight, and right timing. When we meet uncertainty with curiosity instead of fear, we unlock new possibilities and reconnect with the quiet wisdom within. By releasing the urge to push or prove, we align with a more natural rhythm of creation—one that flows from peace, not pressure. In this space, our faith is strengthened, our questions become sacred, and our dreams begin to take form not through force but through harmony, trust, and inner alignment.

UNBALANCED EXPRESSION:

The unbalanced expression of this Mercury retrograde cycle shows up as resistance, control, and the relentless need to figure it all out. Instead of softening into trust, we may spiral into self-doubt, allowing fear to shut down our curiosity and close us off from possibility. In this state, we try to force clarity, push outcomes, or seek external validation, disconnecting from our inner sense of timing and peace. This reactive energy creates tension, disharmony, and exhaustion, keeping us stuck in cycles of overthinking, mistrust, and emotional struggle rather than allowing life to unfold with grace.

CONTEMPLATIONS:

- Where in my life am I still trying to force clarity, timing, or outcomes—and what might happen if I softened my grip and trusted the process instead?
- How does self-doubt show up in my thoughts or choices, and what would it look like to meet that doubt with curiosity instead of fear?
- What parts of me are craving peace—and what needs to be released in order for that peace to emerge from within?
- In what ways have I been narrowing my vision, and how can I reopen to possibility, wonder, and the unknown?
- What would it feel like to trust that everything I need is arriving in perfect timing, even if I can't yet see how?

AFFIRMATION:

I trust the unfolding of my life. I release the need to control, to force, or to rush. I meet my doubt with compassion and my questions with curiosity. I surrender to the timing of the Universe and allow peace to rise within me. What is meant for me is already finding its way. I am held, I am guided, I am becoming.

MARCH 2, 2026

GATE 63: CURIOSITY

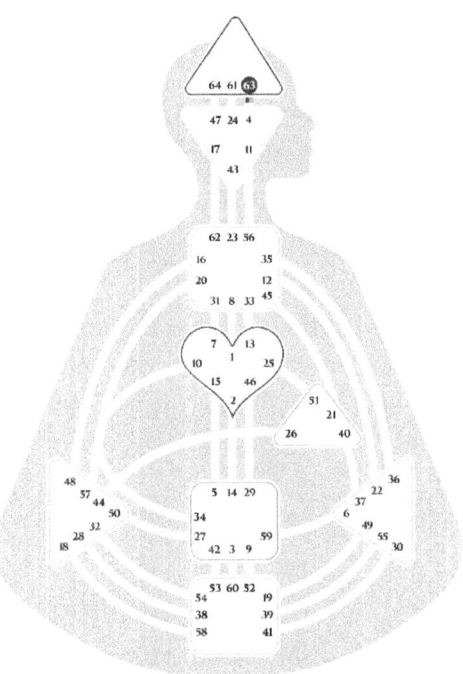

CHALLENGE:

To not let self-doubt and suspicion stop you from being curious.

AFFIRMATION:

My curiosity makes me a conduit of possibility thinking. I ask questions that stimulate imaginations. I allow the questions of my mind to seed dreams that stimulate my imagination and the imagination of others. I share my questions as an opening to the fulfillment of potential in the world.

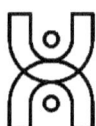
JOURNAL QUESTIONS:

- Am I curious about life?
- Do I regularly allow myself to be curious about what else is possible in the world? In my life?
- Do I doubt myself and my ideas?
- What needs to happen for me to unlock my need to be right about an idea and to allow myself to dream of possibilities again?

EFT SETUP:

Even though I struggle with trusting myself, I now choose to relax and know that I know. I listen to my intuition. I abandon logic and let my higher knowing anchor my spirit in trust, and I deeply and completely love and accept myself.

EARTH:

Gate 64: Divine Transference

How can you embrace your dreams and stop judging them even if you don't know how to yet?

MARCH 3, 2026

FULL MOON AND TOTAL LUNAR ECLIPSE

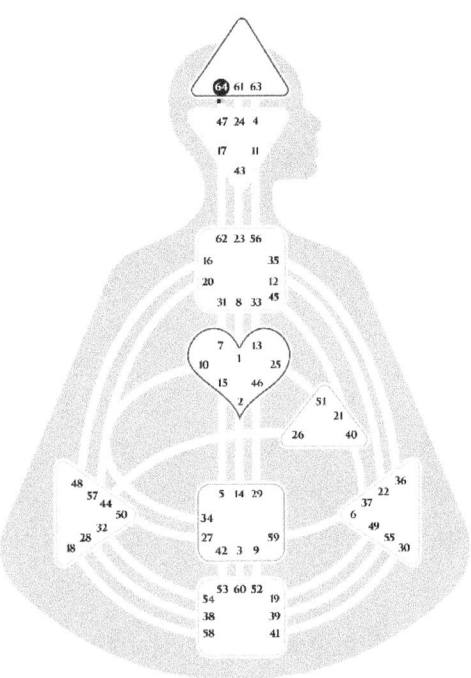

Virgo 12°51'

Gate 64: The Gate of Divine Transference

Full moon energy invites us to explore what we need to release and let go of to stay in alignment with our intentions. Eclipse energy amplifies the intensity of the full moon, giving us an extra boost to let go and release!

The total lunar eclipse on March 3, 2026, occurs in Virgo, activating the Virgo-Pisces axis—a polarity that invites us to harmonize the sacred balance between order and surrender, the rational mind and intuitive flow, structure and spirit. This eclipse is a powerful opportunity to release the limitations of overanalysis, perfectionism, and doubt that can obstruct the full expression of our creative potential. The Virgo moon, in its full brilliance, illuminates where we may be clinging to plans, timelines, or rigid systems that strangle our dreams before they're allowed to take root. The invitation here is to let go of the pressure to know how something will unfold and instead trust the sacred mystery of emergence.

In Quantum Human Design, this full moon eclipse highlights Gate 64, the Gate of Divine Transference. This gate sits at the threshold of inspired vision and initiates the alchemical process of receiving, translating, and embodying divine imagination. When lit by the full moon and intensified through an eclipse, Gate 64 reminds us that the first step to creating the future is allowing ourselves to see it—clearly, wildly, and without apology. This isn't about logic or strategy—it's about imagination as a spiritual act. What are you afraid to imagine? What dreams do you secretly hold but push away because they feel too big, too strange, too uncertain?

The full moon's energy supports deep release, and in this case, it asks us to let go of the conditioned belief that we need a plan before we can dream. This eclipse reveals how often we reject our own desires because they don't yet seem practical or realistic. In doing so, we unconsciously collapse possibility. This lunation reminds us that practicality is not a prerequisite for dreaming—it's often the result of having dreamed first. Releasing the compulsion to immediately figure out the logistics opens us to divine timing, unexpected opportunities, and guidance that unfolds one step at a time.

The Virgo-Pisces axis teaches that true creation requires both devotion and surrender. We are asked to ground our faith in daily practices that keep the dream alive: writing, imagining, meditating, visioning. But we are also called to surrender control over the timeline and outcome. This eclipse offers a gentle but firm nudge to tend the dream, to hold the image of what we long for, and to trust that the how will arrive in perfect time—when we're ready and the path is clear.

Let this full moon be your ceremonial release of doubt. Breathe space into the too-big dreams. Rather than shrinking your vision to fit the known, expand your trust to meet the unknown. The moonlight is a mirror—let it reflect back to you the sacredness of your longings and the worthiness of your wildest hopes.

CHALLENGE:

The big lesson of this eclipse is to release the need to know how your dreams will come to life and instead give yourself full permission to dream without limits. Trust that clarity, timing, and next steps will unfold naturally as you hold the vision with devotion and faith. This is your invitation to stop downsizing your desires and start honoring them as sacred.

OPTIMAL EXPRESSION:

The optimal expression of this eclipse is the ability to merge inspired vision with grounded trust, honoring your dreams as sacred and tending to them with daily devotion while releasing control over the outcome. It's a graceful balance of imagination and surrender, where faith in the unseen becomes the foundation for creating what's truly aligned.

UNBALANCED EXPRESSION:

The unbalanced experience of this eclipse may look like overthinking, perfectionism, or dismissing your dreams because they feel too impractical or overwhelming. You might feel stuck in analysis, trying to control the path instead of trusting the process. This can lead to shrinking your vision or stopping yourself short simply because you don't yet know how to make your dream come true, forgetting that the path is often revealed only after the dream is claimed.

CONTEMPLATIONS:

- What dreams or visions have I been pushing aside because I don't yet know how to bring them to life?
- Where am I trying to control the outcome instead of trusting the process of divine timing and guidance?
- What old beliefs or perfectionistic patterns am I ready to release in order to make space for bigger, bolder dreaming?
- How can I begin to nurture my dreams daily, even if I don't feel ready or have it all figured out?

AFFIRMATION:

I honor my dreams as sacred. I release the need to know how, and I trust that each step will reveal itself in divine timing. I am worthy of dreaming big—and even bigger.

MARCH 8, 2026

GATE 22: SURRENDER

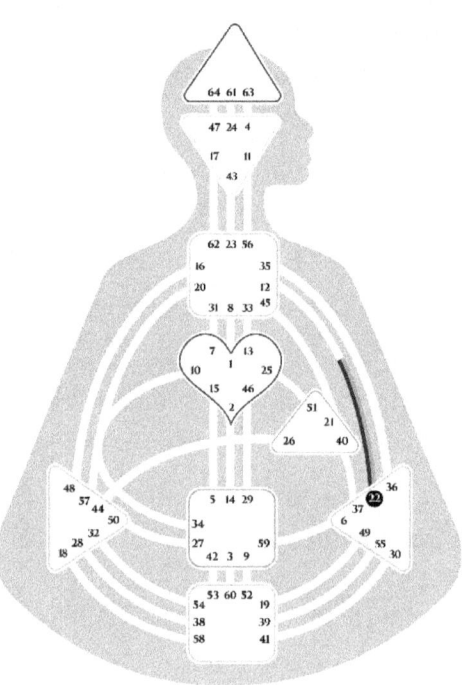

CHALLENGE:

To trust that your passions and deepest desires are supported by the universal flow of abundance. To have the courage to follow your passion and know that you will be supported. To learn to regulate your emotional energy so that you have faith that everything will unfold perfectly.

AFFIRMATION:

I am a global change agent. I am inspired with passions that serve the purpose of transforming the world. I trust that my emotions and my passion will align me with faith and the flow of resources I need to fulfill my life purpose. When I let go and follow my passion, I am given everything I need to change the world.

JOURNAL QUESTIONS:

- Where am I denying my passion in my life? Where have I settled for less than what I want because I'm afraid I can't get what I want?
- What do I need to do to fully activate my passion? What is one bold step toward my genius that I could take right now?
- Do I trust the Universe? What do I need to do to deepen my trust?
- Do I have a regular practice that supports me in sustaining a high frequency of emotional energy and alignment?
- What needs to be healed, released, aligned, and brought to my awareness for me to deepen my faith?

EFT SETUP:

Even though it is hard to trust in my support, I now choose to trust anyway, and I deeply and completely love and accept myself.

EARTH:

Gate 47: Mindset

How can you cultivate more hope and optimism? This week, practice enjoying all your ideas for the sake of enjoying them without the expectation that you need to figure out how to turn those ideas into reality.

MARCH 13, 2026

GATE 36: EXPLORATION

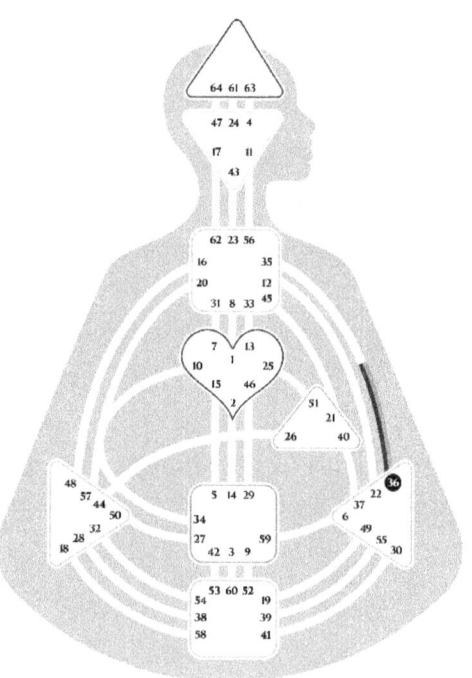

CHALLENGE:

To not let boredom cause you to leap into chaos. To learn to stick with something long enough to become skillful and to bear the fruits of your experience.

AFFIRMATION:

My experiences and stories break old patterns and push the boundaries of the edge of what is possible for humanity. I defy the patterns, and I create miracles through my emotional alignment with possibility. I hold my vision and maintain my emotional energy as I wait to bear the fruit of my intentions and my visions.

JOURNAL QUESTIONS:
- How does boredom impact my life? What do I do when I feel bored? What can I do to keep myself aligned even when I'm bored?
- What stories have I experienced that have shattered old patterns and expectations? How have my stories changed or inspired others?
- What do I do to maintain or sustain emotional alignment? What do I need to add to my daily practice to amp up my emotional energy around my intentions?

EFT SETUP:
Even though it is scary to be out of my comfort zone, I now choose to push myself into something new and more aligned with my truth, and I deeply and completely love and accept myself.

EARTH:
Gate 6: Impact

Contemplate how you feel about abundance. List all the different ways you have been abundantly supported in the past.

MARCH 19, 2026

GATE 25: SPIRIT

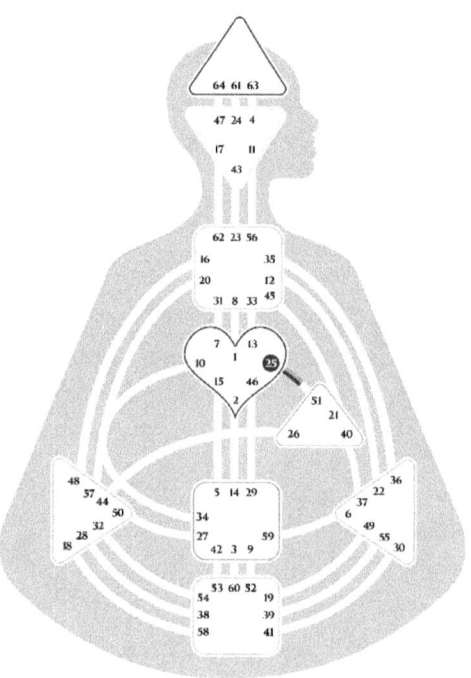

CHALLENGE:

To trust the divine order in all of your life. To learn to connect with Source as the path to creating well-being in your life. To remember that your life serves an irreplaceable role in the cosmic plan and to honor that role and to live from it. To trust Source.

AFFIRMATION:

I am an agent of the Divine. My life is the fulfillment of divine order and the cosmic plan. When I am connected to Source, I serve my right place. I take up no more than my space and no less than my place in the world. I serve, and through serving, I am supported.

JOURNAL QUESTIONS:
- Do I trust Source?
- Do I have a regular practice that connects me to Source?
- Do I know my life purpose?
- Am I living true to my purpose?
- How can I deepen my connection to my purpose?

EFT SETUP:
Even though in the past, I was afraid to follow my heart, I now choose to do what is right for me and know that I am fully supported, and I deeply and completely love and accept myself.

EARTH:
Gate 46: Embodiment

What do you need to do to better love and nurture your body? This week spend some time in front of the mirror and ask your body what it needs to embody greater vitality.

MARCH 19, 2026

NEW MOON

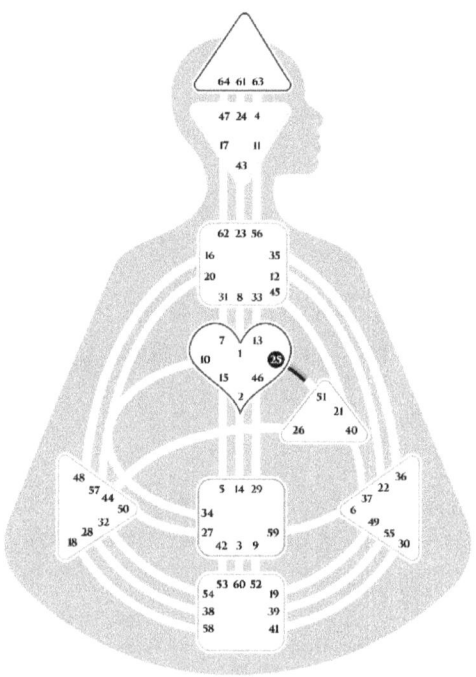

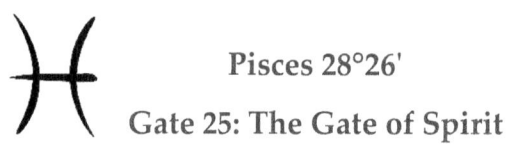

Pisces 28°26'

Gate 25: The Gate of Spirit

New moon energy invites us to explore how we can deepen our alignment with our intentions and asks us to focus on what we want to grow and expand on in our lives.

The March 19, 2026, new moon is a powerful and sacred invitation to begin again—this time, in radical alignment with your higher purpose. Illuminating Gate 25, the Gate of Spirit in Quantum Human Design, this lunar cycle calls you into the deepest recesses of your heart to reclaim your connection to Source, to remember who you truly are, and to initiate a new chapter of life led by authenticity, truth, and service. This is not just a personal new beginning—it is a spiritual reorientation that asks you to realign your choices, your actions, and your presence in the world with your soul's unique path.

Gate 25 teaches us that purpose is not something we find—it is something we embody. It lives within us, pulsing beneath the noise of expectation and conditioning, waiting to be remembered and lived. This new moon brings the energetic momentum to proclaim your inherent value—not for validation but as a declaration of readiness to serve from a place of wholeness.

To fully live your purpose, you must believe that you are worthy of being resourced, supported, and sustained in your mission. When you claim your value, you also claim the right to be nourished and empowered by life itself.

The energy of Gate 25 can be profoundly expansive and healing. It reconnects you to a frequency of unconditional love—first for yourself and then as a vessel for the world. When you live aligned with your higher purpose, you become a channel for grace, a living reminder of what's possible when we trust the intelligence of the heart. This new moon is an initiation into that grace, a moment to root into your sacred why and allow it to guide every next step. You don't have to know the full path ahead. You only have to commit to walking it with faith and integrity.

In its shadow expression, this energy can feel hollow, lonely, or even existential. You may feel untethered from meaning or question whether you truly belong. Doubt, disillusionment, or spiritual fatigue can surface, revealing where you've lost trust—in life, in others, or in yourself. But these questions are not signs of failure. They are the doorway. If you're willing to sit with them, they will point you back to what is real. This new moon asks: What would shift if you believed—truly believed—that your life has purpose? That you are here on purpose? That your being is a sacred contribution to the world?

CHALLENGE:

To optimize the energy of this new moon, you must learn to trust in your inherent worth and claim your value as the foundation for living your higher purpose. This is a time to release the illusion of purposelessness and anchor yourself in the truth that your life is divinely guided, deeply meaningful, and essential to the greater whole.

OPTIMAL EXPRESSION:

The optimal expression of this new moon is a deep, embodied alignment with your higher purpose, rooted in unconditional self-worth and trust in divine support. From this place, you serve the world with authenticity, clarity, and a profound sense of spiritual wholeness.

UNBALANCED EXPRESSION:

The unbalanced experience of this new moon may feel like spiritual disconnection, purposelessness, or a loss of faith in your path and inner guidance. You might struggle with self-doubt, question your worth, and feel unsupported or uncertain about why you're here.

CONTEMPLATIONS:
- Where in my life am I being called to remember and reclaim my higher purpose?
- What old stories or beliefs about my worth must I release in order to serve from a place of truth and love?
- How do I experience connection—or disconnection—with Source, and what practices help me return to that connection?
- What would it look like to fully trust that I am here on purpose and that my presence is enough?
- In what ways am I being invited to offer my gifts in service to something greater than myself?

AFFIRMATION:
I am a vessel of divine purpose, fully worthy, fully supported, and guided by the wisdom of my heart. I trust that my life has meaning, and I am ready to embody and express my highest truth.

MARCH 25, 2026

GATE 17: ANTICIPATION

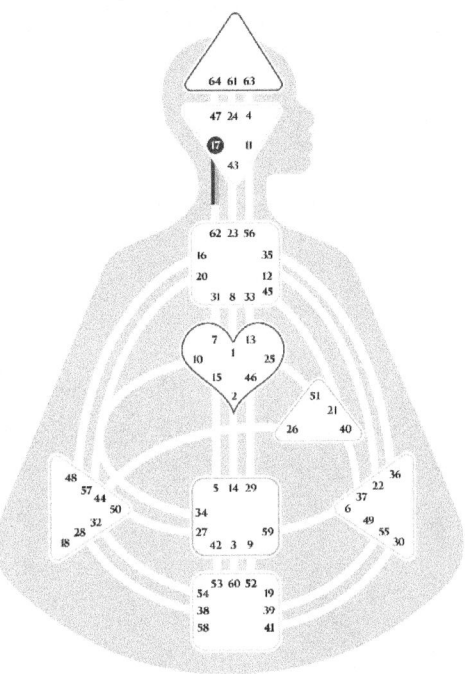

CHALLENGE:

To learn to share your thoughts about possibilities only when people ask for them. To not let doubt and suspicion keep you from seeing the potential of positive outcomes.

AFFIRMATION:

I use the power of my mind to explore possibilities and potential. I know that the inspirations and insights that I have create exploration and experimentation that can inspire the elegant solutions necessary to skillfully control the challenges facing humanity.

JOURNAL QUESTIONS:
- What do I need to do to manage my insights and ideas so that they increase the options and potential of others?
- How do I feel about holding back from sharing my insights until the timing is right?
- What can I do to manage my need to share without waiting for the right timing?
- What routines and strategies do I need to cultivate to keep my perspectives expanding and possibility oriented?
- How can I improve my ability to manage doubt and fear?

EFT SETUP:
Even though I have a lot of ideas and thoughts to share, I trust that the insights I have to offer are too important to blurt out, so I wait for the right people to ask, and I deeply and completely love and accept myself.

EARTH:
Gate 18: Re-Alignment

This week explore where you need to add more joy to your life. Do you have any old stories you need to release around being "right?"

MARCH 30, 2026

GATE 21: SELF-REGULATION

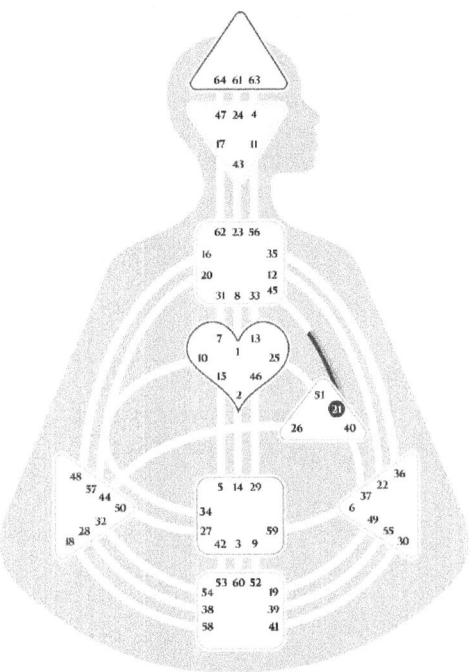

 **CHALLENGE:**
To learn to let go. To become proficient at self-regulation. To release the need to control others and circumstances. To trust in the Divine and to know that you are supported. To know that you are worthy of support and that you don't have to overcompensate.

 **AFFIRMATION:**
I am worthy of claiming, protecting, and defending my rightful place in the world. I create an inner and outer environment that is self-generous, and I regulate my environment to sustain a high frequency of alignment with my true value. I know that I am an irreplaceable and precious part of the cosmic plan, and I create my life to reflect the importance of my right place in the world.

JOURNAL QUESTIONS:
- Where do I need to release control in my life?
- Do I trust the Universe?
- Do I value myself? Do I trust that I will be supported in accordance with my value?
- What do I need to do to create an internal and external environment of self-generosity?
- What needs to be healed, released, aligned, and brought to my awareness for me to embrace my true value?

EFT SETUP:
Even though in the past I felt like I had to control everything, I now surrender to Source and know that my abundance, my true abundance, is available to me when I let go and let the Universe do the work, and I deeply and completely love and accept myself.

EARTH:
Gate 48: Wisdom

Make a list of all of your trainings, all of the skills you have, and all of the knowledge you've gleaned from your life experiences. Take some time to truly acknowledge what you know.

APRIL 2, 2026

FULL MOON

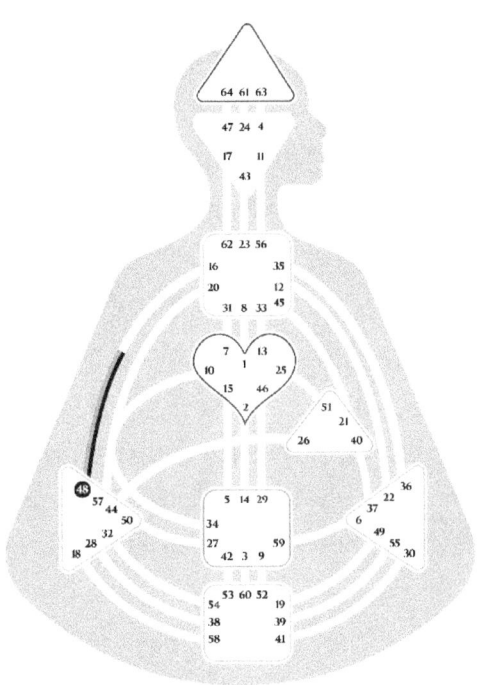

Libra 12°20'

Gate 48: The Gate of Wisdom

Full moon energy invites us to explore what we need to release and let go of to stay in alignment with our intentions.

The April 2, 2026, full moon illuminates Gate 48, the Gate of Wisdom, in the Quantum Human Design chart. As always, full moons ask us to look honestly at what needs to be released—what is keeping us from fulfillment and alignment. This particular lunation turns our attention inward, toward the stories we tell ourselves about whether we are ready, qualified, or enough. Gate 48 asks us to acknowledge the deep well of wisdom we have accumulated through life's lessons, lived experience, and intentional learning. This is not textbook knowledge—it is embodied truth. We are being asked to shine a light on where we still question our own authority and to let go of the fear that we are not yet prepared to meet our higher calling.

In its shadow expression, Gate 48 can stir up a nagging sense of inadequacy—a haunting worry that we're not smart enough, credentialed enough, or prepared enough to show up fully. This can manifest as perfectionism, overconsumption of information, or hesitation in the face of uncertainty. The fear of the unknown can lead us to overeffort in an attempt to create safety through control. But no amount of research will ever eliminate uncertainty. The deeper invitation of this moon is to shift our trust from the mind to the body, from strategy to inner wisdom, and from fear to faith.

Aligned with the earlier new moon in Gate 25, the Gate of Spirit, this full moon forms a powerful partnership. Gate 25 reminded us to reconnect with our higher purpose—to remember that we are not here by accident. This full moon now invites us to clear out the internal clutter that says we are not enough to fulfill that purpose. It's a sacred moment to release the resistance that keeps us from embodying our spiritual role as a vessel for wisdom in the world. When we trust that we have enough and are enough, we allow ourselves to serve in greater alignment and integrity.

This moon brings a profound opportunity for integration. You are not lacking—you are being asked to see yourself clearly. The call is not to gather more knowledge but to stand rooted in the truth you already carry. Let this full moon be a reckoning with your own readiness, a shedding of false narratives, and a quiet but powerful return to the wisdom that lives within you. When you release the fear of inadequacy, you become a wise guide—not because you know everything, but because you have learned to trust what you know.

CHALLENGE:

To optimize this full moon energy, you must trust that the wisdom you've already earned is enough. The lesson is to release the fear of inadequacy and stop seeking external proof of your readiness. Fulfillment comes not from knowing more, but from honoring what you already know and allowing it to guide you forward.

OPTIMAL EXPRESSION:

The optimal expression of this full moon energy looks like quiet confidence rooted in lived experience and inner knowing. It shows up as a willingness to share your wisdom without overexplaining, to act without needing permission, and to trust that your timing is divinely aligned. You move with clarity, not because you have all the answers but because you trust the value of your perspective—and you know that your presence, as it is now, is enough.

UNBALANCED EXPRESSION:

The unbalanced expression of this full moon energy shows up as fear-driven striving—an obsessive need to gather more knowledge, prove your worth, or prepare for every possible unknown. It can manifest as perfectionism, procrastination, or chronic self-doubt that keeps you stuck in overanalysis instead of aligned action. At its core, it's a disconnection from your inner wisdom and a belief that you are not yet enough to fulfill your purpose.

CONTEMPLATIONS:

- Where in my life am I still waiting to feel ready before I allow myself to act, speak, or share?
- What life experiences have shaped the wisdom I carry today?
- What stories have I inherited or internalized that tell me I must know more or be more to be worthy of fulfillment?
- In what ways might I be using the pursuit of knowledge as a distraction from embodying what I already know?
- If I truly believed I was wise enough right now, how would I show up differently?

AFFIRMATION:

I trust the wisdom I carry. I am enough, I know enough, and I am ready now to embody the fullness of my purpose.

APRIL 5, 2026

GATE 51: INITIATION

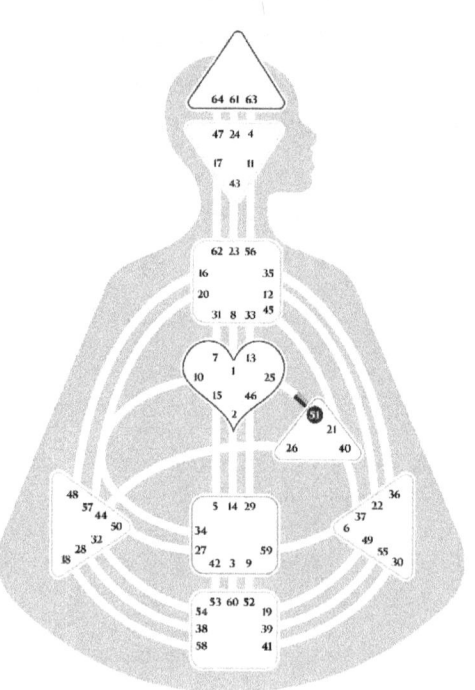

CHALLENGE:
To not let the unexpected cause you to lose your faith. To not let a pattern of unexpected events cause you to lose your connection with your purpose and Source. To learn to use the power of your own story of initiation to initiate others into fulfilling their rightful place in the cosmic plan.

AFFIRMATION:
I navigate change and transformation with grace. I know that when my life takes a twist or a turn, it is my soul calling me out to serve at a higher level. I use disruption as a catalyst for my own growth and expansion. I am a teacher and an initiator. I use my ability to transform pain into growth and power to help others navigate through crisis and emerge on the other side empowered and aligned.

JOURNAL QUESTIONS:
- What has shock and the unexpected taught me in my life?
- How can I deepen my connection to Source?
- How can my experiences of initiation be shared with others? What am I here to wake people up to?

EFT SETUP:
Even though things are not turning out like I expected, I now choose to embrace the unexpected and trust that the Universe is always serving my greater good, and I deeply and completely love and accept myself.

EARTH:
Gate 57: Instinct

Notice your intuition this week. What does your intuition feel like to you? Sometimes doing a retrospective analysis of your intuition and instinct makes it more clear how your intuitive signals work.

APRIL 11, 2026

GATE 42: CONCLUSION

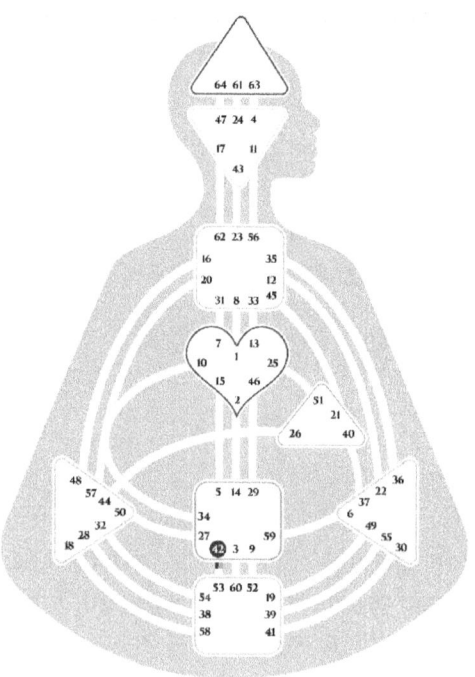

CHALLENGE:

To learn to bring things to completion. To allow yourself to be led to where you need to be to finish things. To value your ability to know how to finish and to learn to give up your need to try to start everything. To finish things in order to create space for something new.

AFFIRMATION:

I am gifted at knowing when and how to finish things. I respond to bringing events, experiences, and relationships to a conclusion in order to create space for something new and more abundant. I can untangle the cosmic entanglements that keep people stuck in old patterns. My ability to realign and complete things helps others create space for transformation and expansion.

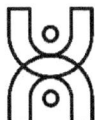

JOURNAL QUESTIONS:

- Do I own and value my natural gift of knowing how to bring things to completion?
- What things in my life do I need to finish to make room for something new?
- Am I holding on to old circumstances and patterns because I'm afraid to let them go?
- Do I judge myself for not starting things? How can I learn to be gentler with myself?

EFT SETUP:

Even though I have hesitated in the past to finish what I needed to finish in order to make room for something new and better, I now choose to bring things to a powerful ending. I know that I am taking strong action to create space for what I truly want to create in my life, and I deeply and completely love myself.

EARTH:

Gate 32: Endurance

What actionable steps do you need to complete to be ready for creating what you want? Do one thing to lay the foundation for your dreams this week.

APRIL 16, 2026

GATE 3: INNOVATION

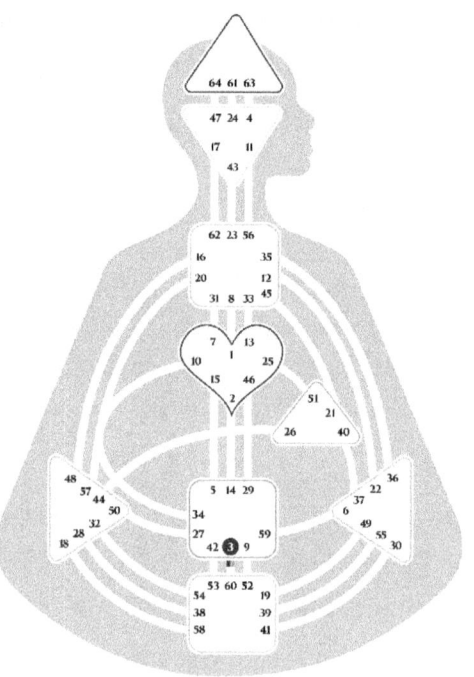

 **CHALLENGE:**

To learn to trust in divine timing and to know that your ideas and insights will be transmitted to the world when the world is ready.

 **AFFIRMATION:**

I am here to bring change to the world. My natural ability to see what else is possible to create something new is my strength and my gift. I patiently cultivate my inspiration and use my understanding of what is needed to help evolve the world.

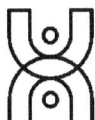
JOURNAL QUESTIONS:
- Do I trust in divine timing?
- Where has divine timing worked out in my life? What has waiting taught me?
- If the opportunity to share my ideas with the world presented itself today, would I be ready? If not, what do I need to prepare to be ready?

EFT SETUP:
Even though it is scary to take the first step, I now trust the Universe and my ability to be innovative and know that I stand on the cusp of the fulfillment of my big dreams. I deeply and completely love and accept myself.

EARTH:
Gate 50: Nurturing

This week practice taking care of yourself first—without guilt—so that you can better take care of others!

APRIL 17, 2026

NEW MOON

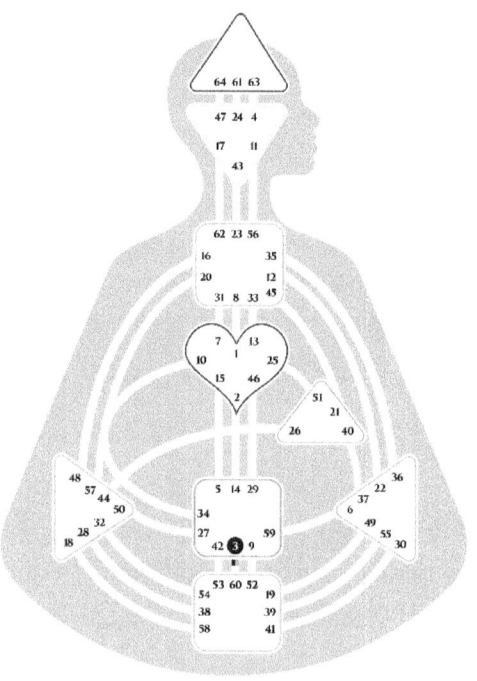

Aries 27°28'

Gate 3: The Gate of Innovation

New moon energy invites us to explore how we can deepen our alignment with our intentions and asks us to focus on what we want to grow and expand on in our lives.

The April 17, 2026, new moon ushers in a potent moment of growth, particularly in how we evolve, create, and innovate. Occurring in Gate 3, the Gate of Innovation in Quantum Human Design, this lunation offers a powerful opportunity to explore how we bring the new into form. Innovation in this context is not born from chaos or complete reinvention—it emerges from the clarity and wisdom of what is already working. This is not about abandoning what has gotten us here but about refining it, expanding it, and building upon it with discernment. The key is to honor the present while opening to what's possible next.

This moon teaches us that authentic innovation holds a deep respect for what came before. It asks us to take stock of what is currently functioning in our lives—our systems, our relationships, our creativity—and to bless those things with gratitude. But this is not gratitude that asks us to settle or stop reaching. Instead, it is a dynamic, active gratitude that becomes the fertile ground for expansion. Gate 3 reminds us that it is not only possible but necessary to hold gratitude and desire simultaneously. We are allowed to want more, to dream bigger, and to evolve beyond the limits of our current reality—even as we appreciate what is.

There is a subtle pressure in this new moon energy—a push toward the new, the next, the not-yet-known. This pressure can be exhilarating or destabilizing, depending on how we meet it. If we leap into change without anchoring in what we know, without respecting the foundation we're building on, we risk bypassing the wisdom of experience. The shadow of Gate 3 is mutation without structure—change for change's sake, experimentation without roots. While experimentation has value, sustainable innovation requires a bridge between what is and what's becoming. That bridge is built with gratitude, discernment, and strategic creativity.

As we set intentions under this new moon, we are invited to ask: What is already working in my life? What foundations can I honor and expand upon? How can I hold space for both appreciation and longing? This is a moon for creating from wholeness, not lack. It reminds us that our next step doesn't have to erase the past—it can be a continuation, an elevation, a conscious choice to build something visionary from what is already good, already true, already alive.

CHALLENGE:
The lesson of this new moon is that true innovation begins with honoring what already works. It teaches us to hold both gratitude and desire—to appreciate the present while courageously reaching for what's next. Growth doesn't require starting over; it requires building with intention, wisdom, and trust in the unfolding.

OPTIMAL EXPRESSION:
The optimal experience of this new moon is one of grounded expansion—feeling deeply grateful for what is while inspired by the possibilities of what could be. It's a moment of creative clarity, where innovation flows from a solid foundation and desire is guided by wisdom. This is a time to confidently build the new by honoring and evolving the best of the old.

UNBALANCED EXPRESSION:
The shadow of this new moon may show up as restless urgency to change for the sake of change—discarding what's working in pursuit of something unproven or prematurely new. It can manifest as a rejection of gratitude, mistaking dissatisfaction for desire, and mistaking disruption for innovation. Without honoring the foundation, we risk building on instability rather than wisdom.

CONTEMPLATIONS:

- What in my life is already working well, and how can I build upon it with intention and care?
- In what ways might I be confusing gratitude with settling?
- What am I longing for that feels like an authentic next step, not a rejection of the present?
- How can I honor the wisdom of past experiences while opening to new, innovative possibilities?
- Where am I being called to trust the process of growth, even if I can't yet see the full outcome?

AFFIRMATION:

I honor what is working in my life and trust in my power to expand it. I am rooted in gratitude and open to inspired innovation.

APRIL 22, 2026

GATE 27: ACCOUNTABILITY

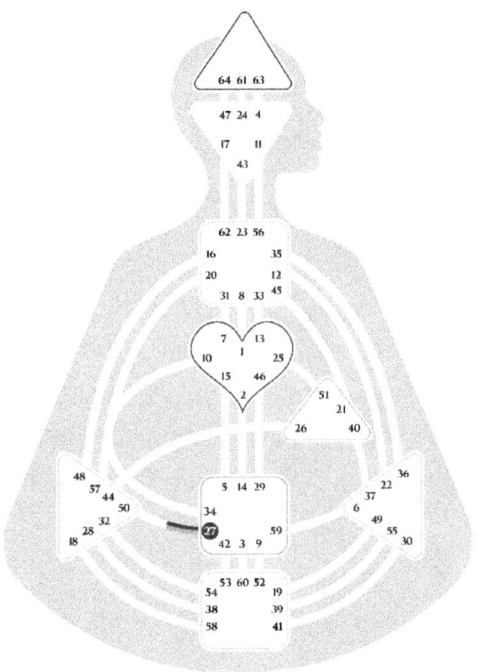

CHALLENGE:

To care without overcaring. To allow others to assume responsibility for their own challenges and choices. To learn to accept other people's values. To not let guilt cause you to compromise what is good and right for you.

AFFIRMATION:

I have a nurturing and loving nature. It is my gift to be able to love and care for others. I know that the greatest expression of my love is to treat others as capable and powerful. I support when necessary, and I let go with love so my loved ones can discover their own strength and power.

JOURNAL QUESTIONS:
- Am I taking responsibility for things that aren't mine to be responsible for? Whose problem is it? Can I return the responsibility for the problem back to its rightful owner?
- What role does guilt play in motivating me? Can I let go of the guilt? What different choices might I make if I didn't feel guilty?
- What obligations do I need to set down for me to take better care of myself?
- Are there places where I need to soften my judgments of other people's values?

EFT SETUP:
Even though it is hard to say no, I now choose to take the actions that are correct for me. I release my guilt, and I deeply and completely love and accept myself.

EARTH:
Gate 28: Challenge and Adventure

Where do you need to cultivate a sense of adventure in your life? Do one adventurous thing this week!

APRIL 28, 2026

GATE 24: BLESSINGS

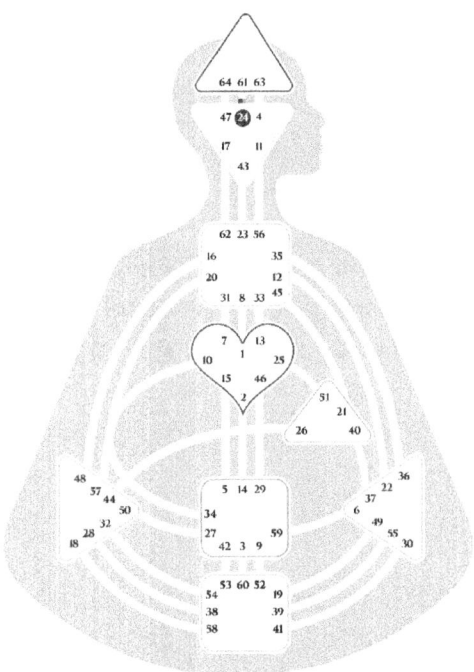

CHALLENGE:
To learn to allow what you truly deserve in your life. To not rationalize an experience that allowed for less than you deserve. To find the blessings and power from painful experiences and to use them as catalysts for transformation.

AFFIRMATION:
I embrace the mystery of life with the awareness that the infinite generosity of the Universe gives me blessings in every event in my life. I find the blessings from the pain. I grow and expand beyond the limitations of my experiences and stories. I use what I have learned to create a life and circumstances that reflect the miracle that I am.

JOURNAL QUESTIONS:
- What are the blessings I learned from my greatest painful experiences? Can I see how these experiences served to teach me? What did I learn?
- What am I grateful for from the past?
- Where might I be rationalizing staying stuck or settling for less than what I really want or deserve? What do I need to do to break out of this pattern?

EFT SETUP:
Even though it is scary to start something new… I am afraid I am not ready… I now choose to courageously embrace the new and trust that everything is in divine order, and I deeply and completely love and accept myself.

EARTH:
Gate 44: Truth

What patterns from the past are holding you back from allowing yourself to see and embody your true worth? What old patterns do you need to release this week?

MAY 1, 2026

FULL MOON

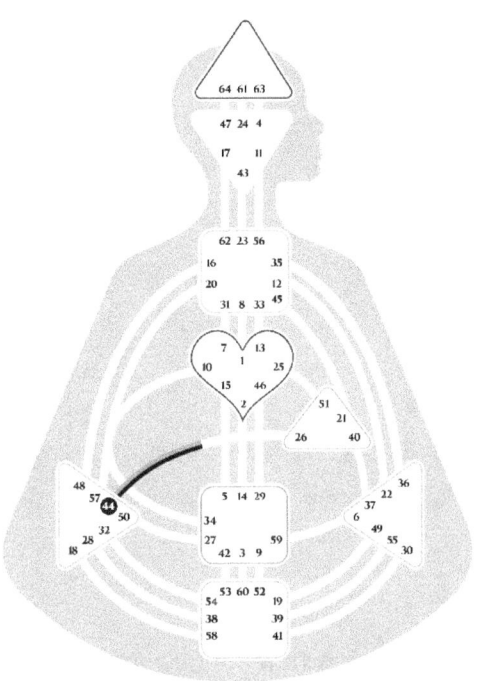

♏ Scorpio 11°20'

Gate 44: The Gate of Truth

Full moon energy invites us to explore what we need to release and let go of to stay in alignment with our intentions.

The May 1, 2026, full moon invites us to illuminate the patterns that linger beneath the surface—those ingrained responses and inherited fears that were once protective but now limit our growth. This full moon highlights Gate 44, the Gate of Truth in Quantum Human Design, an energy that compels us to recognize what from the past is still shaping our choices today. We are being asked to examine where we may be reacting from old wounds instead of responding from wisdom. These reactive patterns—formed to keep us safe—often mask our deeper truth, and until we become aware of them, they quietly sabotage our efforts to live in alignment with our value.

This is a powerful moment of reckoning. The Gate of Truth asks us not only to witness the patterns we carry but also to have the courage to release them. We are not meant to fear the return of past pain or trauma but to meet those echoes with awareness and compassion. Full moons are always a time for release, and this one asks us to release the unconscious belief that history will inevitably repeat itself. When we hold on too tightly to the fear of the past, we shape our present through avoidance rather than intention. Now is the time to interrupt those cycles and reclaim the freedom to choose something new.

Gate 44 helps us discern truth—not just objective truth but the personal truth that is rooted in value, integrity, and self-worth. If we are still filtering our present through the lens of outdated beliefs or survival mechanisms, we can't fully step into our personal power. This moon brings us a chance to call our energy back from the past, to draw a clear line between what was and what is, and to shift our awareness to the truth of who we are becoming. In doing so, we heal not by denying the past, but by refusing to let it dictate our future.

This full moon beautifully complements the April new moon, which brought the energy of innovation through Gate 3. If the new moon asked us to build something new, this full moon asks us to clear the space to do so without dragging our old fears into the foundation. We cannot innovate while looking backward. We cannot evolve while gripping stories that no longer serve us. This is a lunar threshold—an invitation to release the fear of repetition so that we may meet the unknown with clarity, intention, and courage. Let the past bless you but not bind you. Let the light of this moon reveal the truth, and let that truth set you free.

CHALLENGE:

The lesson of this full moon is to recognize and release the fear-based patterns of the past that keep you from living in alignment with your truth and value. It's a call to move forward with courage and integrity, no longer letting old wounds shape your future.

OPTIMAL EXPRESSION:

The optimal expression of this full moon's energy is the courageous release of reactive patterns rooted in fear, allowing you to respond to life with clarity and self-trust. It's the embodiment of truth and integrity, when you honor the lessons of the past without letting them define you. From this space, you step into the future with grounded confidence and a deep alignment with your value.

UNBALANCED EXPRESSION:

The unbalanced expression of this full moon's energy can show up as fear-driven reactivity, where past wounds distort present truth and lead to self-sabotage or mistrust. It may also manifest as avoidance—ignoring or bypassing the past instead of learning from it—which keeps old patterns repeating. In either case, we remain stuck, unable to move forward with clarity, confidence, or integrity.

CONTEMPLATIONS:

- What recurring patterns from your past continue to influence how you see yourself and make decisions today?
- Where do you feel fear that history will repeat itself, and how does that fear shape your actions?
- In what ways have you been reacting to protect yourself rather than responding from your truth?
- What truths about your value and integrity are ready to be seen more clearly under the light of this full moon?
- What might become possible if you release the belief that your past defines your future?

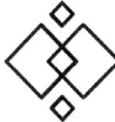
AFFIRMATION:

I release the patterns of the past with compassion and clarity, and I stand rooted in my truth, guided by courage, integrity, and the wisdom of who I am becoming.

MAY 4, 2026

GATE 2: ALLOWING

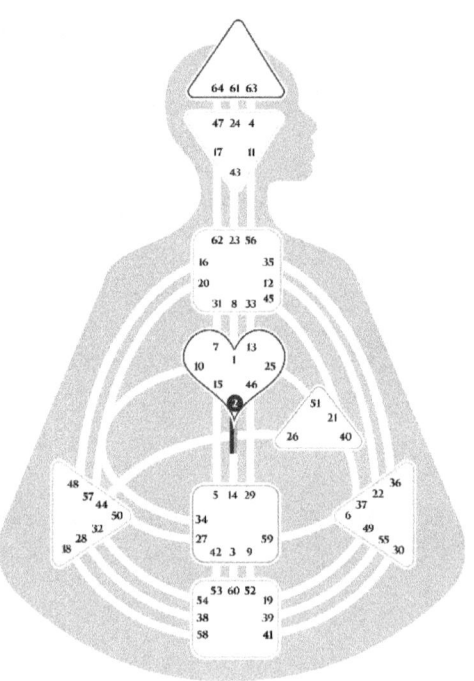

CHALLENGE:

To love yourself enough to open to the flow of support, love, and abundance. To incrementally increase over the course of your life what you're willing to allow yourself to receive. To learn to know that you are valuable and lovable simply because you exist.

AFFIRMATION:

I allow myself to receive the full flow of resources and abundance I need to fully express all of who I am. I recognize that my life is a vital, irreplaceable part of the cosmic tapestry, and I receive all that I need because it helps me contribute all that I am.

JOURNAL QUESTIONS:

- Do I ask for help when I need it? Why or why not?
- Do I trust the Universe/God/Spirit/Source to support me in fulfilling my intentions?
- Am I grateful for what I have? Make a list of everything I'm grateful for.
- Can I transform my worry into trust?
- Do I believe that I deserve to be supported?

EFT SETUP:

Even though I am scared because nothing looks like I thought it would, I now choose to relax, trust, and receive the support that I am designed to receive. I know that I will be supported in expressing my true self, and I deeply and completely love and accept myself.

EARTH:

Gate 1: Purpose

Spend time this week thinking about your purpose and the gifts you long to give the world. How aligned are you with your purpose?

MAY 9, 2026

GATE 23: TRANSMISSION

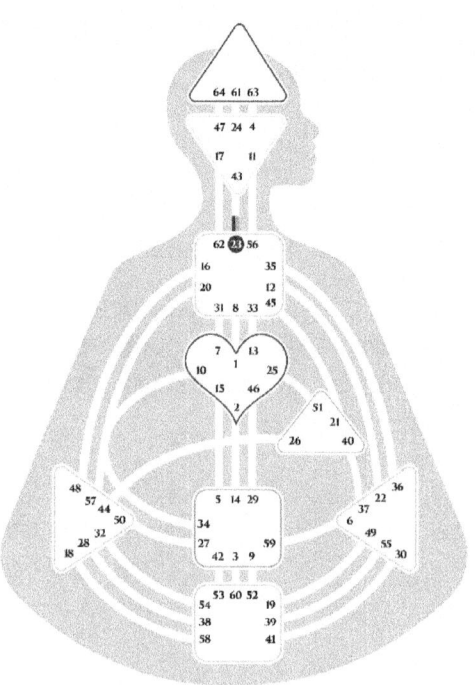

CHALLENGE:

To recognize that change and transformation are inevitable. To know what needs to happen next, to wait for the right timing and the right people to share your insights with. To not jump the gun and try to convince people to understand what you know. To not let yourself slip into negativity and despair when people aren't ready.

AFFIRMATION:

I change the world with what I know. My insights and awarenesses have the ability to transform the way people think and perceive the world. I know that my words are powerful and transformative. I trust that the people who are ready for the change that I bring will ask me for what I know. I am a vessel for my knowingness, and I nurture myself while I wait to share what I know.

JOURNAL QUESTIONS:
- How can I strengthen my connection to Source?
- Do I trust what I know? What comes up for me when I know something, but I don't know how I know what I know?
- How do I handle myself when I know something but the people around me aren't ready to hear it yet?

EFT SETUP:
Even though in the past I shut down my voice, I now speak my truth and offer the contribution of my unique spirit to the world, and I deeply and completely love and accept myself.

EARTH:
Gate 43: Insight

This week you're learning to trust your knowingness. Practice trusting your inner knowing and the thoughts and ideas you have. Watch for self-doubt and don't discount what you know even if you don't know how you know what you know.

MAY 15, 2026

GATE 8: FULFILLMENT

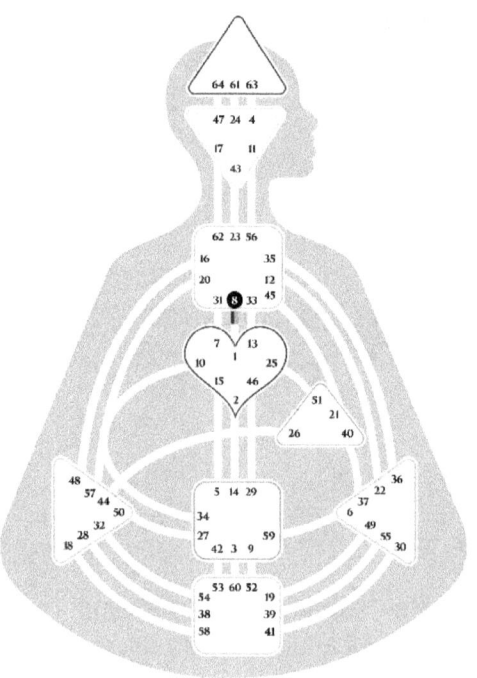

 **CHALLENGE:**

To learn to express yourself authentically. To wait for the right people to see the value of who you are and to share yourself with them, with vulnerability and through all your heart. To learn to trust that you are a unique expression of the Divine with a purpose and a path. To find that path and to walk it without self-judgment or holding back.

 **AFFIRMATION:**

I am devoted to the full expression of who I am. I defend and protect the story of my life. I know that when I am expressing myself, without hesitation or limitation, I am the contribution that I am here to give the world. Being myself is my life purpose, and my direction flows from my authentic alignment.

JOURNAL QUESTIONS:

- Do I feel safe being vulnerable?
- What experiences have caused me to feel unsafe expressing my true self? Can I rewrite those stories?
- What would an uncompromising life look like for me?
- What do I need to remove from my current life to make my life more authentic?
- What is one bold action I can take right now that would allow me to express who I am more authentically in the world?
- What is my true passion? What do I dream of?

EFT SETUP:

Even though I question whether I have something of value to add to the world, I now choose to courageously follow the whispers of my soul and live a life that is a powerful expression of the truth of who I am. I speak my truth. I value my contribution. I know I am precious, and I deeply and completely love and accept myself.

EARTH:

Gate 14: Creation

Ask yourself this week, "If I didn't need the money, what work would I be doing?" How is this work showing up in your life right now?

MAY 16, 2026

NEW MOON

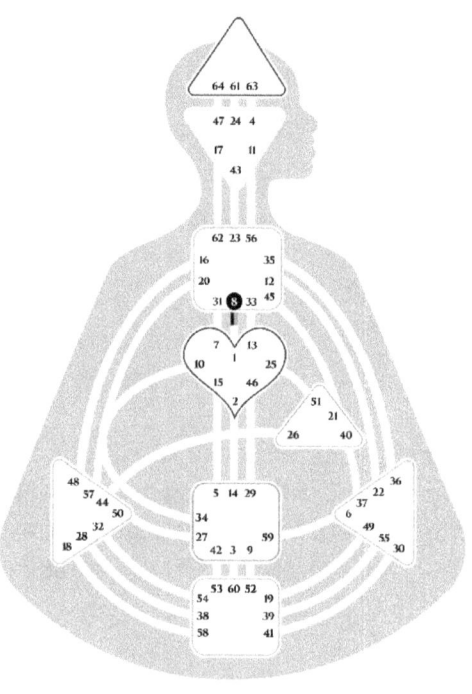

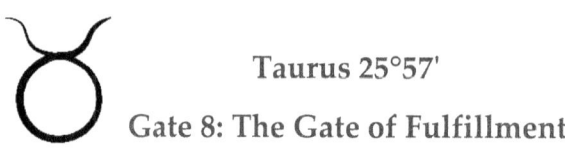

Taurus 25°57'

Gate 8: The Gate of Fulfillment

New moon energy invites us to explore how we can deepen our alignment with our intentions and asks us to focus on what we want to grow and expand on in our lives.

The May 16, 2026, new moon offers a powerful invitation to begin again—this time with a renewed devotion to being unapologetically yourself. New moons bring us the energy of reset and intention-setting, encouraging us to pause and recalibrate our creative trajectory. With this new moon activating Gate 8, the Gate of Fulfillment in Quantum Human Design, the cosmos calls us inward to align our next steps not with external pressures or outcomes but with the essence of who we truly are. This is a potent moment to reorient your creative direction around the truth of your being rather than the productivity of your doing.

Gate 8 reminds us that our ultimate fulfillment comes not from what we accomplish but from how courageously and fully we embody our authenticity. This gate lives in the Activation Center (Throat), where voice becomes vibration and vibration shapes reality. It urges us to express the unique story that only we can tell, to live from the heart, and to trust that being deeply, wholly ourselves is not only enough—it is the very reason we exist. Our power lies in our presence, and our presence becomes magnetic when it is aligned with truth.

This new moon brings an invitation to deepen your connection to your inner voice, to refine your self-expression, and to explore where you may still be holding back or conforming out of fear, habit, or the desire to belong. It challenges you to ask whether you are living in a way that reflects the fullness of your essence or whether you've been dimming your light to fit into someone else's mold. The energy of Gate 8 doesn't demand performance—it asks for presence, heart-led integrity, and a willingness to stand in your originality even when it feels vulnerable or uncertain.

As you plant seeds under this new moon, consider how your intentions can be shaped by devotion to your truest self. This is a time to express your creative energy in ways that feel nourishing and liberating. Trust that your authentic self is not only worthy of expression—it is essential to the evolution of the whole. Your story matters. Your voice has power. And your fulfillment is not a destination—it's a way of being, lived moment by moment, in alignment with the heart.

CHALLENGE:

The core lesson of this new moon cycle is to remember that true fulfillment comes from expressing who you are—not proving what you can do. You are here to live your story, not someone else's, and your authenticity is the very gift the world needs now. This cycle invites you to stop hiding, start speaking your truth, and trust that your presence is your purpose.

OPTIMAL EXPRESSION:

The optimal expression of this new moon energy is a bold, heart-led authenticity that radiates from the inside out. It looks like living your truth without apology, expressing your unique voice with clarity and conviction, and trusting that simply being who you are is enough to inspire, influence, and create. When aligned, this energy turns your life into a living work of art—original, magnetic, and deeply fulfilling.

UNBALANCED EXPRESSION:

The unbalanced expression of this new moon energy can manifest as self-doubt, conformity, or silencing your voice to gain approval or avoid rejection. It may show up as chasing fulfillment through external achievements while feeling disconnected from your true self. In this state, you risk living a version of your life that looks successful on the outside but feels hollow and misaligned within.

CONTEMPLATIONS:

- What parts of myself have I been hiding to feel safe or accepted?
- Where am I still trying to prove my worth instead of embodying my truth?
- What does fulfillment feel like when I let go of external expectations?
- How can I honor the story that only I am here to live and express?
- What would it look like to speak from the heart without fear of how I'll be received?

AFFIRMATION:

I honor the truth of who I am and express it with courage, clarity, and heart. My authenticity is my purpose, and my presence is my power.

MAY 21, 2026

GATE 20: PATIENCE

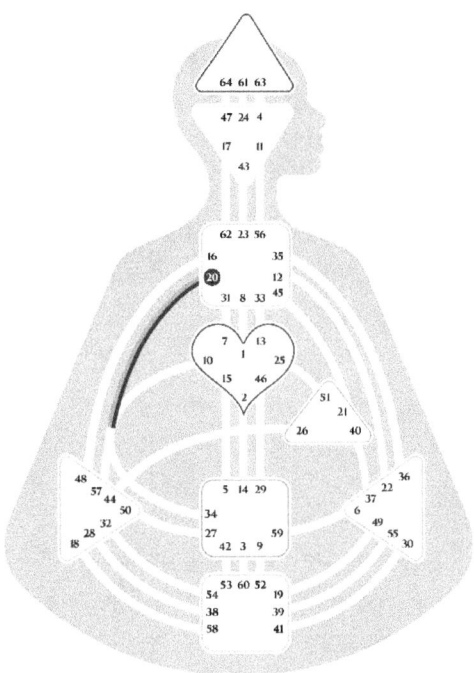

CHALLENGE:

To be patient and control the ability to wait. To be prepared and watchful but resist the urge to act if the timing isn't right or if there are details that still need to be readied.

AFFIRMATION:

I am in the flow of perfect timing. I listen to my intuition. I prepare. I gather the experience, resources, and people I need to support my ideas and my principles. When I am ready, I wait patiently, knowing that right timing is the key to transforming the world. My alignment with right timing increases my influence and my power.

JOURNAL QUESTIONS:
- How do I manage my need for action? Am I patient?
- Do I trust in divine timing? Do I trust my intuition?
- What needs to be healed, released, aligned, and brought to my awareness for me to trust my intuition?

EFT SETUP:
Even though it is scary to not do anything and wait, I now choose to trust the infinite abundance of the Universe, and I deeply and completely love and accept myself.

EARTH:
Gate 34: Power

How can you cultivate greater patience while you're waiting? What fears come up for you when you think of waiting? How can you learn to wait with patience and ease and see right timing as power?

MAY 27, 2026

GATE 16: ZEST

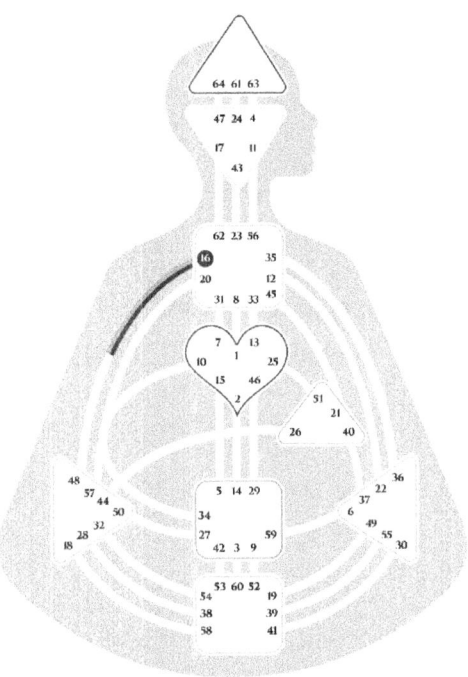

CHALLENGE:

To learn to temper your enthusiasm by making sure you are prepared enough for whatever it is you are trying to do or create.

AFFIRMATION:

I am a faith-filled, contagious force. I take guided actions, and I trust my intuition and awareness to let me know when I am prepared and ready to leap into expanding my experience and genius. My enthusiasm inspires others to trust in themselves and to take their own giant leaps of growth.

JOURNAL QUESTIONS:

- Do I trust my gut?
- Do I need to slow down and make sure I've done my homework before I take action?
- Have I sidelined my enthusiasm because other people have told me that I cannot do what I am dreaming of doing?

EFT SETUP:

Even though I am afraid that I am not fulfilling my life purpose and that I am wasting my life, I now choose to relax and know that I am in the perfect place at the perfect time to fulfill my destiny, and I deeply and completely love and accept myself.

EARTH:

Gate 9: Convergence

This week, explore your physical environment and ask yourself if there is something in your environment that is distracting you from your focus. What can you do to improve your environment? What can you do to increase your focus?

MAY 31, 2026

FULL MOON

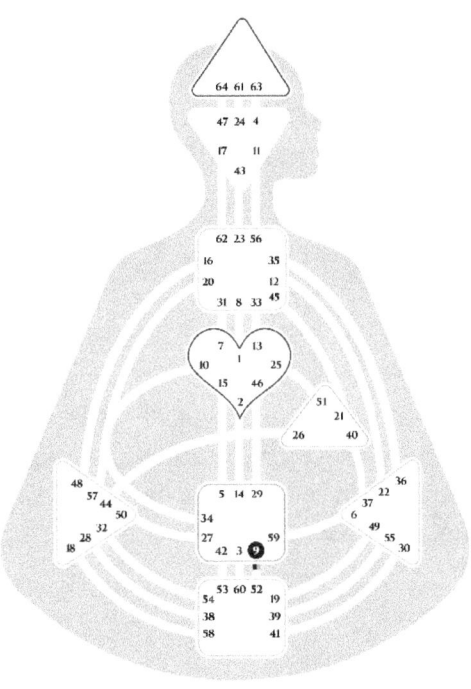

Sagittarius 9°55'

Gate 9: The Gate of Convergence

Full moon energy invites us to explore what we need to release and let go of to stay in alignment with our intentions.

The May 31, 2026, full moon arrives as a rare blue moon, casting an amplified spotlight on what needs to be healed, released, or brought into alignment. This lunation illuminates Gate 9 in Quantum Human Design—the Gate of Convergence. Known as the energy of focus, this gate asks us to examine how and where we are directing our precious attention. Full moons bring clarity, and this one offers the gift of discernment. It beckons us to notice whether we're channeling our energy into purposeful, aligned action—or scattering it in ways that drain and dilute our creative power.

The Gate of Convergence teaches that focus is not about rigidity or control—it's about intentionality. When we are aligned with our deeper vision and sense of purpose, focus becomes a powerful tool of manifestation. This full moon encourages us to recalibrate our energetic investments and to choose, with clarity and consciousness, what is worthy of our attention. We are reminded that our energy is sacred and that how we use it determines what we create.

If we've been spinning in overwhelm, pulled in too many directions, or seduced by distractions that pull us off course, this full moon offers a moment of reckoning. It invites us to gently but firmly refocus, to come home to our center, and to remember the importance of discernment. Are we pursuing what truly matters, or are we responding to urgency, noise, and the demands of others? This moon helps us clear out the clutter—energetic, emotional, mental—and realign with the path that is most resonant with our soul's blueprint.

Ultimately, this is a moon of empowerment through clarity. The convergence of our energy—when gathered with focus and purpose—becomes a potent force for change. This full moon is not only a call to release the distractions, but also a sacred reminder to trust that our energy, when fully aligned, is enough to move mountains.

CHALLENGE:

The lesson of this full moon is the power of focused energy. It invites us to release distractions, realign with what truly matters, and become more intentional in where we place our attention. When we converge our energy with clarity and purpose, we unlock the potential for meaningful, aligned progress.

OPTIMAL EXPRESSION:

The optimal expression of this full moon is clear, grounded focus fueled by purpose and intention. It looks like consciously choosing where to direct your energy, saying no to distractions, and aligning your actions with your deeper vision. In this state, your efforts become precise, powerful, and deeply impactful.

UNBALANCED EXPRESSION:

The unbalanced experience of this full moon may feel like mental fog, scattered energy, or an overwhelming sense of being pulled in too many directions. You might find yourself busy but unproductive, chasing distractions, or struggling to prioritize what truly matters. Without clear focus, your energy may be drained by noise rather than channeled toward meaningful outcomes.

CONTEMPLATIONS:
- Where in my life am I investing energy without a clear return or deeper sense of purpose?
- What distractions am I ready to release in order to reclaim my focus?
- What vision or goal feels most aligned with my soul right now—and am I prioritizing it?
- How does it feel in my body when I'm truly focused versus when I'm scattered?
- What boundaries or structures could support me in directing my energy more intentionally?

AFFIRMATION:
I focus my energy on what truly matters, releasing distractions and aligning with the clarity of my purpose.

JUNE 2, 2026

GATE 35: EXPERIENCE

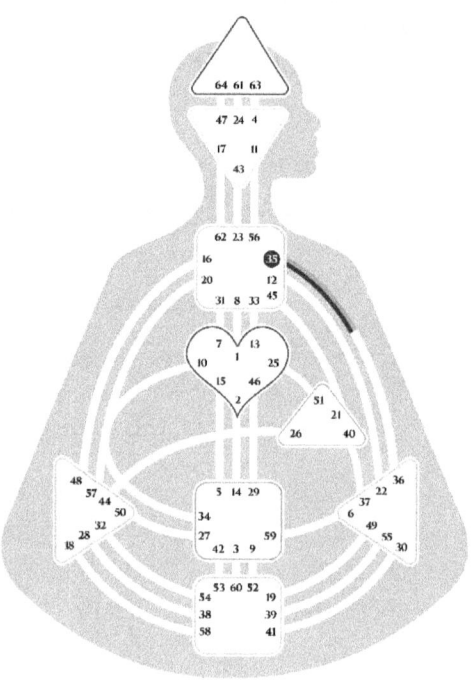

CHALLENGE:

To not let experience lead to feeling jaded or bored. To have the courage to share what you know from your experience. To know which experiences are worth participating in. To let your natural ability to become accomplished at anything keep you from being enthusiastic about learning something new. To embrace that even though you know how to know, you don't know everything.

AFFIRMATION:

I am an experienced, wise, and knowledgeable resource for others. My experiences in life have added to the rich tapestry that is the story of humanity. I share my stories with others because my experiences open doorways of possibility for others. My stories help others create miracles in their lives.

JOURNAL QUESTIONS:

- Where am I finding passion in my life? Do I need to create or discover more passion in my life right now?
- Do I share my knowledge and the stories of my experiences? Do I see the value of what I have to share?
- What am I curious about? How can I expand on that curiosity?

EFT SETUP:

Even though in the past I struggled to stay focused and move forward, I now trust myself to take the next steps on manifesting my dream. I am focused, clear, and moving forward, and I deeply and completely love and accept myself.

EARTH:

Gate 5: Consistency

Do something symbolic this week that represents establishing order in your life. Clean a closet, sort through your purse or wallet. It is a good week to take stock of your habits and explore what habits might need a little refreshing or tweaking.

JUNE 8, 2026

GATE 45: DISTRIBUTION

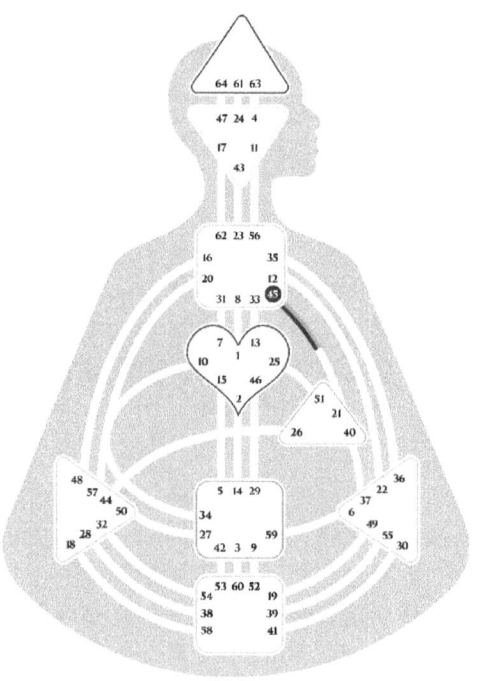

CHALLENGE:

To share and use your resources for the greater good of the whole. To learn to manage resources judiciously so that they benefit the greatest number of people. To teach as a pathway of sharing.

AFFIRMATION:

I am a teacher and a leader. I use my resources, my knowledge, and my experience to expand the resources, knowledge, and experiences of others. I use my blessings of abundance to increase the blessings of others. I know that I am a vehicle of wisdom and knowledge. I sense when it is right for me to share who I am and what I know with others.

JOURNAL QUESTIONS:

- Do I like to share? What do I have to give the world?
- How do I own my right leadership? Am I comfortable as a leader?
- Do I shrink from leadership? Do I overcompensate by pushing too hard with my leadership?
- Do I trust that when the right people are ready, I will be pressed into action as a leader and a teacher?
- What do I need to heal, release, align, or bring to my awareness to trust my leadership energy more?

EFT SETUP:

Even though I'm afraid to look at my finances, I now choose to take a real look at my financial numbers and know that awareness is the first step to increasing my financial status, and I deeply and completely love and accept myself.

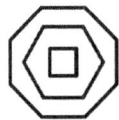

EARTH:

Gate 26: Integrity

Where might you be experiencing a breach in your moral, identity, physical, resource, or energetic integrity? What do you need to do to bring yourself back into integrity?

JUNE 14, 2026

GATE 12: THE CHANNEL

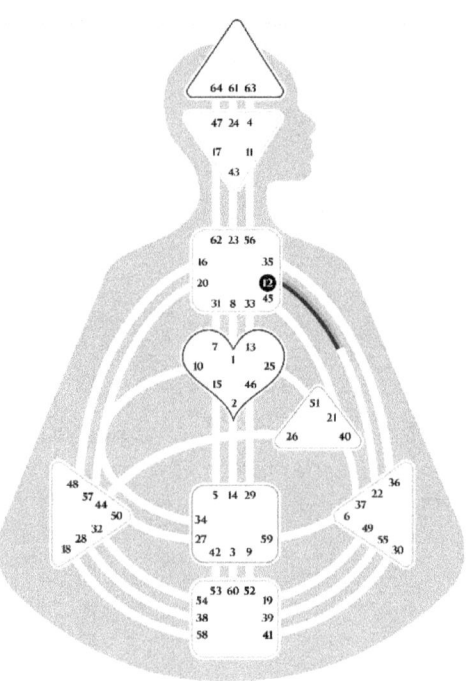

CHALLENGE:

To honor the self enough to wait for the right time and mood to speak. To know that shyness is actually a signal that the timing is not right to share transformational insights and expressions. When the timing is right, to have the courage to share what you feel and sense. To honor the fact that your voice and the words you offer are a direct connection to Source and that you channel the potential for transformation. To own your creative power.

AFFIRMATION:

I am a creative being. My words, my self-expression, my creative offerings have the power to change the way people see and understand the world. I am a vessel of divine transformation, and I serve Source through the words that I share. I wait for the right timing, and when I am aligned with timing and flow, my creativity cultivates beauty and grace in the world. I am a divine channel, and I trust that the words that I share will open the hearts of others.

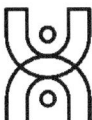

JOURNAL QUESTIONS:

- How has shyness caused me to judge myself?
- What do I need to do to cultivate a deeper connection with Source?
- What do I need to do to connect more deeply with my creative power?

EFT SETUP:

Even though I am afraid that I am failing my life purpose and mission, I now choose to know that I am in the right place fulfilling my right purpose. All I need to do is to follow my strategy, be deliberate, and listen to my heart, and all will be exactly as it needs to be. I deeply and completely love and accept myself.

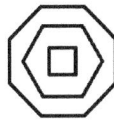

EARTH:

Gate 11: The Conceptualist

Get a blank notebook and train yourself to get into the habit of writing down all your ideas. Nurture these ideas. Dream about them. Fantasize about them and see what shows up in your life in response.

JUNE 15, 2026

NEW MOON

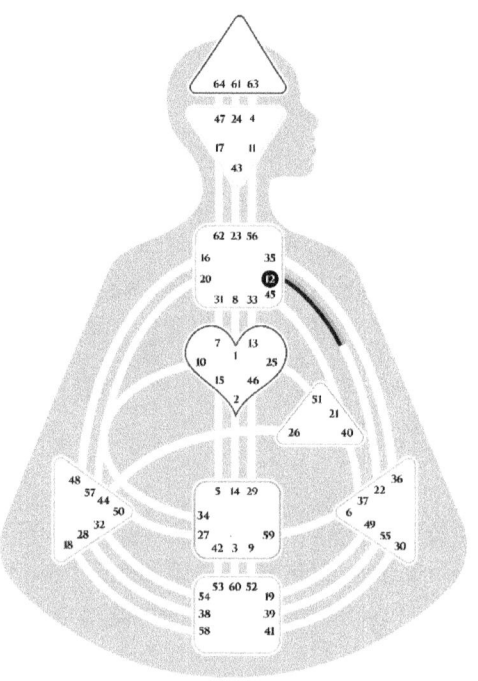

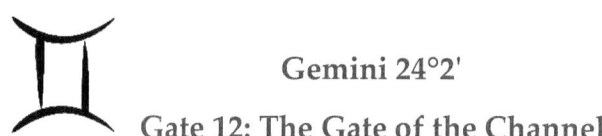 Gemini 24°2'

Gate 12: The Gate of the Channel

New moon energy invites us to explore how we can deepen our alignment with our intentions and asks us to focus on what we want to grow and expand on in our lives.

The new moon on June 15, 2026, invites us into a sacred pause—a moment of stillness where we are called to rededicate ourselves to the creative process, to realign with Source, and to plant seeds for a new beginning. New moons are always a time of inner initiation, but this lunation carries a particularly mystical quality as it highlights Gate 12, the Gate of the Channel in Quantum Human Design. This is a frequency of deep connection to super consciousness, a space where divine inspiration whispers through the veil and reminds us that our creative expression is not just a personal act but a holy transmission.

Gate 12 is not a gate of instant action—it's an energy that teaches us the power of patience and presence. This is a place in the chart where timing is everything. It is not enough to know what we want to express or create; we must also wait for the outer world to open the door for that expression to land, to be received, to ripple. The struggle to find words or the inability to move forward may not be resistance—it may be divine timing protecting the integrity of what wants to be born through us. Trusting this process, even when it feels like delay, is part of the spiritual path this gate offers.

This new moon is an invitation to cultivate inner alignment—to clear our inner channels so that we can be vessels for the messages, creations, and truths that are longing to come through us. When we align our energy with faith and surrender, the channel opens. When we force or push, we often find static and frustration. This lunation asks us to honor the sacred rhythm of creation, to remember that our voice carries not just information, but frequency. And frequency is what shapes form. The clearer our alignment, the more potent our expression becomes.

As you plant intentions under this moon, speak carefully. Choose words that honor the sacredness of your creative power. Allow your voice to become a blessing, both for yourself and for others. Whether you are writing, speaking, praying, or simply dreaming, know that you are engaging in an act of creation that has the power to inspire, uplift, and restructure reality. This is the time to recommit to your channel—to become a vessel for divine timing, holy truth, and inspired possibility.

CHALLENGE:

The lesson of this moon cycle is learning to trust the wisdom of divine timing. If the words won't come or the path isn't clear, it doesn't mean you're unworthy or unprepared—it means the outer world may not yet be ready to receive what's moving through you. This moon teaches us to honor stillness, to wait with faith, and to allow our creative expression to emerge only when both our energy and the moment are fully aligned.

OPTIMAL EXPRESSION:

The optimal expression of this moon's energy is a calm, grounded receptivity to divine inspiration, allowing your voice, truth, and creativity to flow from a place of inner alignment and sacred timing. When you trust the pause and speak with intention, your words become a vessel for healing, vision, and transformation. This is a time to channel, not chase—to let what wants to come through you to emerge with clarity and grace.

UNBALANCED EXPRESSION:

The unbalanced expression of this energy can show up as frustration, self-doubt, or the urge to force communication before the timing is right. It may look like speaking impulsively, oversharing, or withholding your truth out of fear that it won't be received. When disconnected from inner alignment, this energy can feel like emotional pressure without a clear outlet, leading to confusion or creative stagnation.

CONTEMPLATIONS:

- Where in my life am I feeling pressure to speak, act, or create before I feel fully aligned or ready?
- What helps me recognize the difference between divine timing and self-imposed delay?
- How do I experience the presence of Source when I'm quiet, still, and receptive?
- What truths or visions are stirring within me that need time, space, and faith to fully emerge?
- How can I use my words more intentionally—to inspire, uplift, and build what truly matters to me and others?

AFFIRMATION:

I trust the timing of my voice and my creations. I am a clear and sacred channel for divine inspiration, and I allow my truth to emerge with grace, purpose, and power.

JUNE 20, 2026

GATE 15: COMPASSION

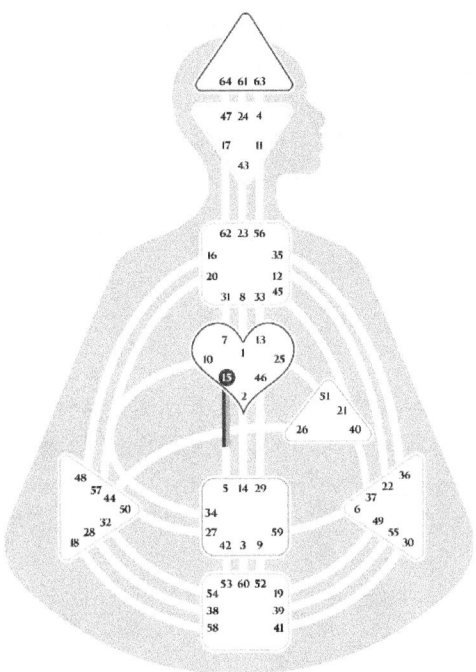

CHALLENGE:
To learn to allow yourself to be in the flow of your own rhythm. To not beat yourself up because you don't have daily habits. To have the courage to do the right thing even if you are worried about not having enough. To share from the heart without giving up your heart and serving as a martyr.

AFFIRMATION:
Like the power of a hurricane to transform the shoreline, my unique rhythm brings change to the landscape of my life and the world around me. I embrace my own rhythm and acknowledge the power of my own heart. I share with ease, and I serve my own heart as the foundation of all I have to give the world.

JOURNAL QUESTIONS:
- Do I trust my own rhythm?
- Do I share from the heart?
- Do I overshare?
- Does my sharing compromise my own heart?
- Do I judge my own rhythm?
- Can I find peace in aligning with my own rhythm?
- What old patterns do I need to break?

EFT SETUP:
Even though I feel powerless to make a difference in the world, I now choose to follow my heart and my passion, knowing that I am the greatest gift I can give the world. The more I show up as my true self, the more I empower others to do the same, and I deeply and completely love and accept myself.

EARTH:
Gate 10: Self-Love

This week focus on nurturing yourself. What can you do to express love and appreciation for yourself?

JUNE 25, 2026

GATE 52: PERSPECTIVE

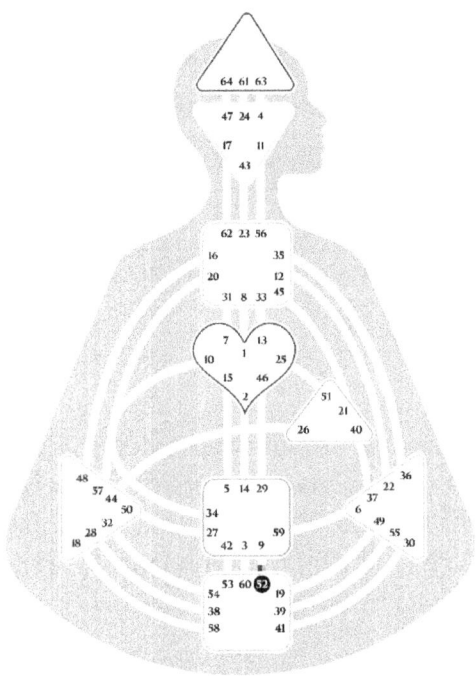

CHALLENGE:

To learn to stay focused even when you're overwhelmed by a bigger perspective. To see the big picture, to not let the massive nature of what you know confuse you and cause you to struggle with where to put your energy and attention.

AFFIRMATION:

I am like the eagle soaring above the land. I see the entirety of what needs to happen to facilitate the evolution of the world. I use my perspective to see my unique and irreplaceable role in the cosmic plan. I see relationships and patterns that others do not always see. My perspective helps us all to build a peaceful world more effectively and in a consciously directed way.

JOURNAL QUESTIONS:

- What do I do to maintain and sustain my focus?
- Is there anything in my environment or my life that I need to move out of the way for me to deepen my focus?
- How do I manage feeling overwhelmed?
- What things am I avoiding because I feel overwhelmed by them?
- What is one bold action I can take to begin clearing the path for action?
- How does my feeling of being overwhelmed affect my self-worth?
- How can I love myself more deeply in spite of feeling overwhelmed?

EFT SETUP:

Even though it makes me nervous to stop doing and sit with the stillness, I now trust the process and know that my state of alignment and clarity with my intentions is the most powerful thing I can do to create effectively and powerfully in my life. I relax, I trust and let my abundance unfold, and I deeply and completely love and accept myself.

EARTH:

Gate 58: Joy

Do at least five things this week simply for the joy of it. Notice how joy feels and commit to cultivating more joy in your daily practice.

JUNE 29, 2026

FULL MOON

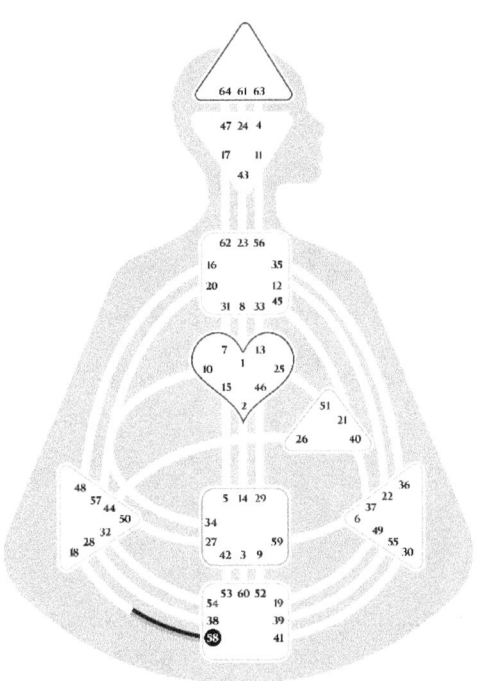

Capricorn 8°14'

Gate 58: The Gate of the Joy of Accomplishment

Full moon energy invites us to explore what we need to release and let go of to stay in alignment with our intentions.

The June 29, 2026, full moon invites us into a powerful moment of illumination and recalibration. As always, full moons cast their light on what has been hidden, buried, or distorted—what must be healed, released, or aligned for us to move forward with greater authenticity and purpose. This particular moon activates Gate 58, the Gate of the Joy of Accomplishment in Quantum Human Design. It's not an emotional kind of joy—it's a deeply energetic one. It is the life-giving fuel that keeps us striving, not out of perfectionism or pressure, but out of an innate drive to grow, refine, and become.

The joy of accomplishment is what keeps us returning to the same practice, not because we must but because something in us loves the process. This gate pulses with the energy of dedication, persistence, and inner enthusiasm. When this joy is alive, it enlivens us from the inside out, helping us press forward—even when the path requires us to go back, revise, or start over. In this light, the full moon reminds us to take an honest look at where our joy may have dimmed and to ask: What beliefs, patterns, or pressures are blocking my joy—and therefore blocking my drive?

For many of us, joy has been sacrificed in the name of practicality. We've been told that success doesn't come from doing what we love or that proficiency must come through struggle and suffering. This moon shines a light on those distortions. It reminds us that true joy is not frivolous—it's a sacred source of power. It is the compass that steers us toward what is meaningful, fulfilling, and ultimately sustainable. Without joy, we burn out. With joy, we endure—and not just endure but thrive.

Under this full moon, we are called to reclaim joy as a necessary ingredient in our evolution. It is not indulgent to want to love what you do—it is essential. This is a moment to release the narratives that have stolen your delight and to realign with the activities, dreams, and pursuits that bring you back to life. When joy is restored, so is your momentum. And with that restored momentum, you are better able to reach for the vision you hold for your life—with passion, purpose, and a steady, radiant fire.

CHALLENGE:

The main lesson of this full moon cycle is that joy is not a luxury—it's a vital source of energy that fuels your success, your motivation, and your sense of meaning. If your drive has been faltering, it may be time to clear what's blocking your joy and reconnect with what truly lights you up. This moon teaches that sustainable success and deep fulfillment begin where joy is allowed to lead.

OPTIMAL EXPRESSION:

The optimal expression of this full moon is a renewed connection to joy as the fuel for your growth, proficiency, and motivation. It invites you to realign with what energizes and inspires you, reminding you that joy and discipline are not opposites—they are partners in your evolution. When joy leads, persistence becomes natural, and success becomes sustainable.

UNBALANCED EXPRESSION:

The unbalanced expression of this energy shows up as burnout, frustration, or a loss of motivation—often because joy has been replaced by pressure, perfectionism, or outdated beliefs about success. You may feel stuck in routines that no longer inspire you, pushing forward without passion or purpose. When joy is suppressed, the drive to grow and evolve weakens, making even small efforts feel heavy and unsustainable.

CONTEMPLATIONS:

- What activities or pursuits naturally bring me a sense of joy, vitality, or quiet enthusiasm—and how often do I make space for them?
- Where in my life have I traded joy for productivity, perfectionism, or external approval?
- What beliefs have I internalized about joy being frivolous or incompatible with success?
- In what area of my life am I craving more energy or motivation—and what joyful practice could I bring into that space?
- What might become possible if I allowed joy to lead my journey toward accomplishment, instead of pressure or fear?

AFFIRMATION:

I honor joy as the fuel for my growth, the guide for my success, and the compass for my success. I release the belief that joy must be earned, and I allow what lights me up to lead the way.

JUNE 29, 2026–JULY 23, 2026

MERCURY RETROGRADE

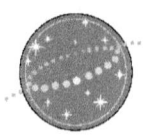

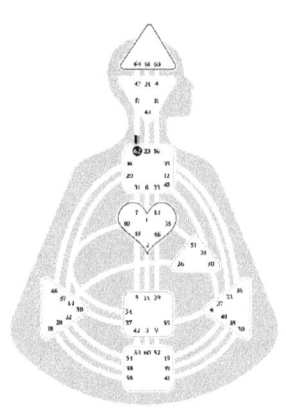

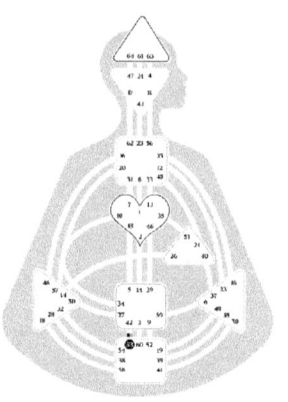

Gate 62

The Gate of Preparation

Gate 53

The Gate of Starting

Retrograde cycles encourage us to go inward to explore the themes the planets give us. Mercury is the planet associated with communication. When Mercury goes retrograde, it gives us an opportunity to go inward and contemplate how we can better align ourselves to have greater influence and impact in the world. Take your time to find the right words during this cycle. Do your best to not make big decisions, sign contracts, or make large purchases. Expect delays. Breathe and be patient with others (and yourself)!

This Mercury retrograde cycle carries a distinct push-me-pull-you dynamic. On one side, we feel the restless urge to begin something new—a spark ignited by Gate 53, the energy of initiation and fresh starts. On the other, we're pulled back by the quieter, more methodical voice of Gate 62, the Gate of Preparation. And, layered over it all, the retrograde motion of Mercury demands inward reflection, pause, and recalibration.

At first glance, this energetic cocktail can feel like being all revved up with nowhere to go. But this is not a mistake—it's an invitation. Gate 62, rooted in the Throat Center, offers a nonmotorized form of readiness: mental clarity, organization, precision in language, and strategic foresight. It is not about action, but about constructing the energetic scaffolding through words, ideas, and mindset. Through this gate, we call in the people, the insights, and the inner alignment needed to move forward—eventually.

Gate 53, too, reminds us that beginnings are sacred and must be timed. It is not about impulsivity or random launching. It asks us to examine whether we have the space, the clarity, and the capacity to sustain what we want to begin. Starting is not simply about movement—it's about readiness, rooted in integrity and alignment.

Together, these gates form a call to clear the stage. This retrograde is less about doing and more about undoing—releasing clutter, untangling lingering thoughts, addressing unfinished business, and making mental and emotional room for what's next. The true preparation now lies in mindset, energetic cleanliness, and clarity of intention.

The challenge of this cycle is resisting the urge to force a premature start. Worry, impatience, and mental clutter can cloud our perception of timing. Frenetic action, if untethered from alignment, will likely lead to frustration and blockages—a common theme in retrograde seasons.

But if we heed the invitation of this cycle—to pause, prepare, and clear the path with purpose—we lay a powerful energetic foundation. And when the timing is right, our next chapter won't just begin; it will unfold with grace.

CHALLENGE:

The core challenge of this Mercury retrograde cycle lies in the pressure to push forward before we're truly ready—a pressure fueled by self-criticism, worry, and mental stress. With the influence of Gate 62, there's a tendency to overanalyze or micromanage our readiness, mistaking mental busyness for true preparation. Gate 53 adds the itch to begin something new, but without the right timing or spaciousness, that urge can turn into anxiety or impulsive action. This tension can lead to a spiral of doubt: questioning whether we've done enough, whether we're falling behind, or whether we're missing our moment. The real work now is resisting that push, calming the inner critic, and trusting that preparation is not always visible—it often begins with mindset, not movement.

OPTIMAL EXPRESSION:

The optimal experience of this Mercury retrograde cycle is one of intentional pause, spacious preparation, and quiet alignment. With Gate 62 offering the power of precise language and mental clarity, and Gate 53 holding the seed of new beginnings, this is a time to build the energetic blueprint for what's next—not through rushed action, but through thoughtful planning, clearing space, and cultivating the right mindset. When we release the pressure to start prematurely and instead focus on organizing our inner and outer world, we create the perfect conditions for authentic momentum to emerge. It's a season of readiness, not rushing—a sacred pause that sets the stage for powerful, aligned action once the timing is right.

UNBALANCED EXPRESSION:

The unbalanced expression of this Mercury retrograde cycle may show up as frantic overthinking, rushing to start something without a clear foundation, and letting fear or self-doubt drive decisions. Under pressure from Gate 62's mental energy, we may become overly critical, obsessing over details or trying to control the unknown through excessive planning or perfectionism. Gate 53's urge to begin can turn into impulsive action—launching projects before we're emotionally, mentally, or energetically prepared. This creates a cycle of frustration, false starts, and burnout. Instead of pausing to align, we may grasp for certainty, push against divine timing, and ultimately sabotage the very beginnings we long to nurture.

CONTEMPLATIONS:

- Where am I mistaking movement for progress, and how can I honor preparation as a powerful form of creation?
- What inner clutter—thoughts, fears, unfinished business—is taking up space I need for something new to emerge?
- How can I use language more intentionally to call in support, alignment, and readiness rather than to reinforce doubt or urgency?
- Am I honoring right timing, or am I pushing from fear, pressure, or the belief that I should be further along?
- What would it feel like to trust that being mentally and energetically ready is just as valuable as taking visible action?

AFFIRMATION:

I trust in divine timing. I prepare with presence, speak with clarity, and create space for what is becoming. I release the need to rush, let go of what no longer serves, and honor the power of alignment over urgency.

JULY 1, 2026

GATE 39: RECALIBRATION

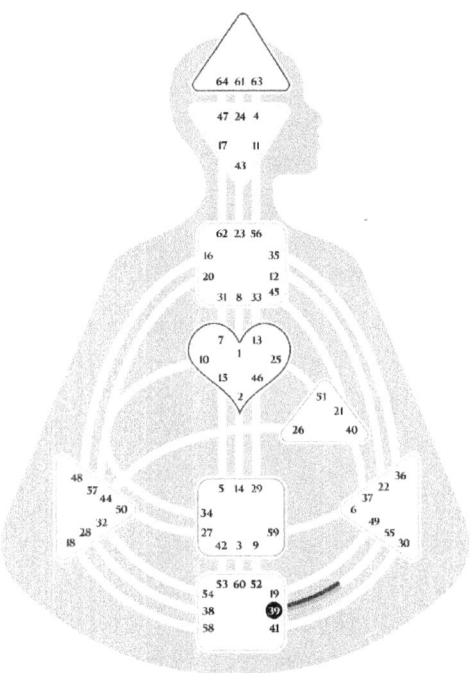

CHALLENGE:

To challenge and tease out energies that are not in alignment with faith and abundance. To bring them to awareness and to use them as pushing off points to deepen faith and trust in Source.

AFFIRMATION:

I am deeply calibrated with my faith. I trust that I am fully supported. I use experiences that create desire and wanting in me as opportunities to deepen my faith that I will receive and create all that I need to fulfill my mind, body, and spirit. I am in the perfect flow of abundance, and I am deeply aligned with Source.

JOURNAL QUESTIONS:
- Do I trust Source?
- What do I need to do to deepen my trust in Source?
- Do I feel like I am enough?
- Do I feel like I have enough?
- Take stock of everything I have and everything I've been given. Do I have enough? Have I ever not been supported?
- What do I have that I'm grateful for?
- Have I abdicated my own power to create?
- What needs to be healed, released, aligned, or brought to my awareness to reactivate my power to create my own abundance?

EFT SETUP:
Even though I worry about money, having the right relationship, and creating abundance in every area of my life, I now trust Spirit and allow the abundant nature of the Universe to reveal itself to me. I stay open to the possibilities of miracles and trust that all I have to do is stay conscious of the abundance of Spirit unfolding within me, and I deeply and completely love and accept myself.

EARTH:
Gate 38: The Visionary

One of the biggest things that can shut you down and cause you to procrastinate is not having a big enough dream. If you were going to blow the edges and limitations off your dream, what would you create with your life? What is your really, really big dream? Spend some time imagining the fulfillment of your dream this week.

JULY 7, 2026

GATE 53: STARTING

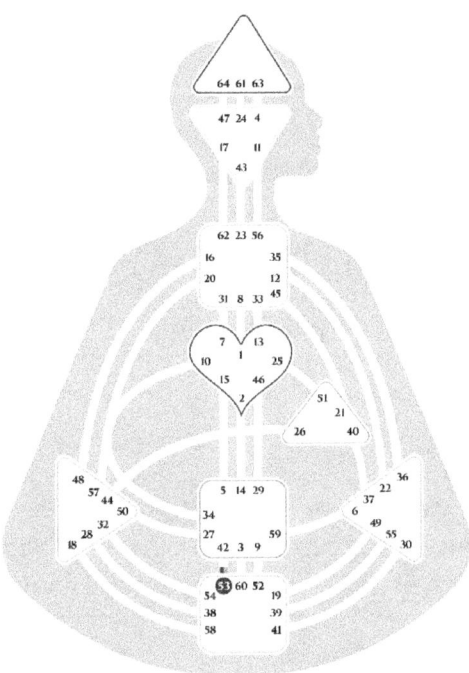

CHALLENGE:

To respond in alignment with your energy blueprint to opportunities to get things started. To initiate the process of preparing or setting the stage for the manifestation of a dream before it becomes a reality. To learn to trust in the timing of the Universe and not take charge and try to implement your own ideas while working against divine timing. To not burn out trying to complete things. To find peace as a starter, not a finisher.

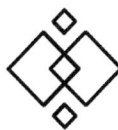

AFFIRMATION:

I am a servant to divine inspiration. My thoughts, inspirations, and ideas set the stage for creative expansion and the potential for evolution. I take action on the ideas that present themselves to me in an aligned way. I honor all other ideas knowing that my gift is in the spark of energy that gets things rolling when the timing is right. While I wait for right timing, I guard my energy and charge my battery so that I am sustainable when the time is right for action.

JOURNAL QUESTIONS:
- How do I feel about myself when I have an idea, and I can't get it initiated?
- How do I feel when someone takes my initial idea and builds on it?
- Do I value what I started?
- What identities and attachments do I have to being the one who starts and finishes something?
- Do I judge myself for not finishing something?
- How can I be gentler with myself?
- Do I trust divine timing?
- How can I deepen my trust in right timing?

EFT SETUP:
Even though I am scared to believe that my big dreams could come true, I now choose to trust the infinite power of the Universe and know that I am never given a dream that can't be fulfilled, and I deeply and completely love and accept myself.

EARTH:
Gate 54: Divine Inspiration

Is there anything you need to do or prepare to be ready for the next step in manifesting your dream or inspiration?

JULY 13, 2026

GATE 62: PREPARATION

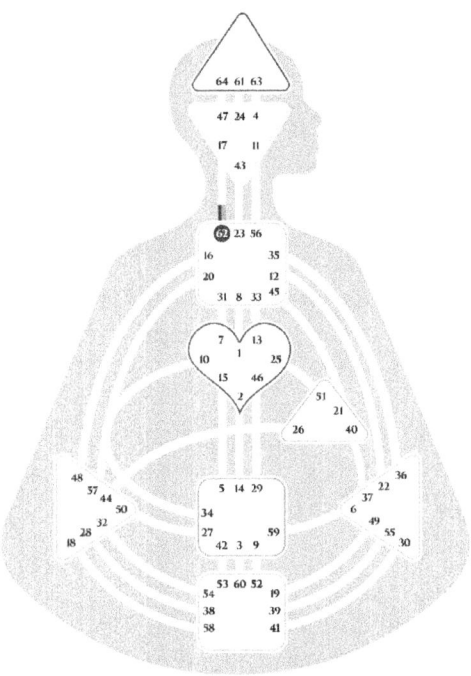

CHALLENGE:

To trust that you will be prepared for the next step. To not let worry and overpreparation distract you from being present in the moment. To not let the fear of not being ready keep you trapped.

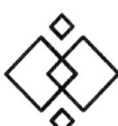
AFFIRMATION:

I create the foundation for the practice of excellence by engineering the plan of action that creates growth. I am in the flow of my understanding, and I use my knowledge and experience to be prepared for the evolution of what is next. I am ready, and I am prepared. I trust my own preparation and allow myself to be in the flow of what is next, knowing that I will know what I need to know when I need to know it.

JOURNAL QUESTIONS:

- Do I worry? What do I do to manage my worry?
- What can I do to trust that I know what I need to know?
- What proof do I have that I am in the flow of preparation?
- Is there anything in my life right now that I need to plan for?
- Am I overplanning? Does my need for contingency plans keep me stuck?

EFT SETUP:

Even though I feel pressure to do something, I now choose to relax and trust the power of my dreams to call the right circumstance to me, and I deeply and completely love and accept myself.

EARTH:

Gate 61: Wonder

This week take some time to look up at the sky. Go somewhere where you can see the stars if possible and gaze at the face of the Cosmos with awe. Bring the feeling of awe into your everyday life.

JULY 14, 2026

NEW MOON

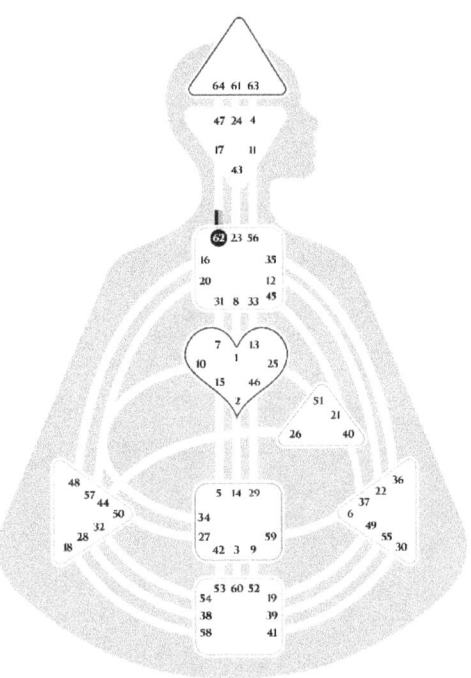

Cancer 21°58'

Gate 62: The Gate of Preparation

New moon energy invites us to explore how we can deepen our alignment with our intentions and asks us to focus on what we want to grow and expand on in our lives.

The new moon on July 14, 2026, invites us into a potent moment of recalibration and renewed intention. As with every new moon, this is a time for planting seeds and resetting our creative compass. With the moon illuminating Gate 62, the Gate of Preparation in Quantum Human Design, we are being asked to turn our attention toward what it really means to be ready. This is a powerful cosmic alignment that encourages us to orient ourselves toward the future—not by rushing to act, but by attuning to the subtle inner signals that guide aligned and effective action.

Gate 62 brings with it a dual resonance of readiness and grounded clarity. It invites us to think clearly, to organize our thoughts and ideas in service to the bigger picture of our intentions. But more importantly, this gate highlights the need for inner alignment before outer action. Preparation, in this context, is not about obsessively planning every detail or hedging against uncertainty. It's about creating inner congruence—clearing self-doubt, releasing old mental patterns, and strengthening our vision so that what we speak and what we see are vibrationally coherent.

This new moon reminds us that much of the work of manifestation begins within. It challenges us to examine how we hold doubt or suspicion in our thinking—especially self-doubt that clouds our ability to perceive what's truly possible. Gate 62 teaches that the moment we begin to see our dreams clearly in the mind's eye, we begin to build the energetic blueprint for those dreams to take form. That clarity generates confidence and receptivity, not because we have all the answers but because we trust the process of revelation and timing.

The shadow of this gate, however, can express as overpreparation rooted in anxiety. It may show up as a compulsive need to figure it all out or to brace ourselves for every possible contingency, especially the worst-case scenario. This can create stagnation, overthinking, and burnout. The lesson of this moon is to loosen our grip on certainty and trust that the right information, resources, and opportunities will emerge when needed. True preparation is about staying open, focused, and ready to respond—not from fear, but from deep alignment with what's unfolding.

CHALLENGE:

The big lesson of this new moon cycle is that true preparation begins with inner alignment, not frantic action. Rather than trying to control every outcome or plan for every possibility, this moon invites us to trust that clarity, insight, and the next right steps will reveal themselves in divine timing. When we clear self-doubt and attune our vision to our creative intentions, we naturally become ready for what's next.

OPTIMAL EXPRESSION:

The optimal expression of this new moon energy is grounded clarity paired with calm, confident readiness. It looks like aligning your thoughts and intentions with your creative vision, trusting that you'll receive the exact insight or information you need, right when you need it. From this place of inner coherence, your actions become precise, purposeful, and in harmony with your greater direction.

UNBALANCED EXPRESSION:

An unbalanced experience of this new moon energy might feel like mental pressure, overthinking, or obsessively trying to plan for every possible outcome. It can manifest as anxiety, doubt, or a frantic need for certainty, making it hard to trust the unfolding process. In this state, preparation becomes a coping mechanism for fear rather than a conscious alignment with intention.

CONTEMPLATIONS:

- What inner shifts do I need to make to truly feel ready for the next step in my creative journey?
- In what ways might fear or self-doubt be distorting my ability to see my vision clearly?
- Am I trying to control the outcome, or am I trusting the timing and wisdom of the unfolding process?
- What practical steps can I take to bring my thoughts and intentions into greater alignment?
- Where in my life am I preparing from a place of anxiety rather than grounded clarity—and what would it feel like to shift into trust?

AFFIRMATION:

I trust that I am becoming ready in perfect timing. With clarity, confidence, and inner alignment, I prepare myself to receive and create what I am truly here for.

JULY 19, 2026

GATE 56: EXPANSION

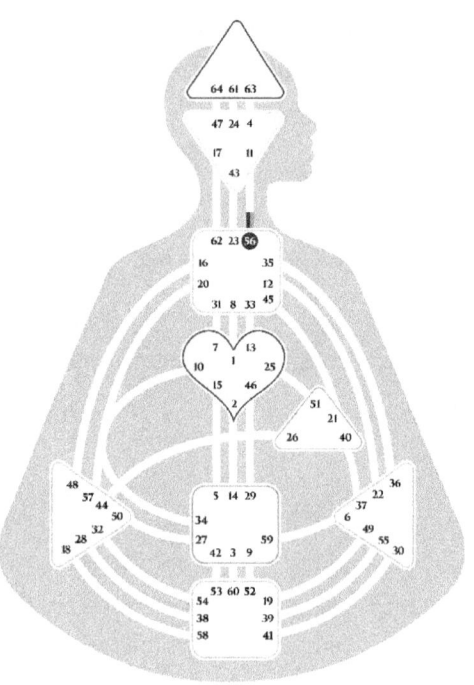

CHALLENGE:

To learn to share stories and inspirations with the right people at the right time. To learn to tell stories of expansion and not of depletion and contraction.

AFFIRMATION:

I am a divine storyteller. The stories of possibility that I share have the power to inspire others to grow and expand. I use my words as a template for possibility and expansion for the world. I inspire the world with my words.

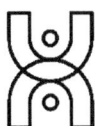
JOURNAL QUESTIONS:
- What stories do I share repeatedly with others?
- Do they lift people up or cause them to contract?
- What stories do I tell about myself and my voice that cause me to either expand or contract?
- What am I here to inspire others to do or be?

EFT SETUP:
Even though I'm afraid to share my ideas, I now choose to take leadership with my inspirations and share my precious ideas with others, and I deeply and completely love and accept myself.

EARTH:
Gate 60: Conservation

Gratitude is the gateway to transformation. This week, take stock of everything in your life that is good and that is working. Make a daily list of the things you're grateful for.

JULY 25, 2026

GATE 31: THE LEADER

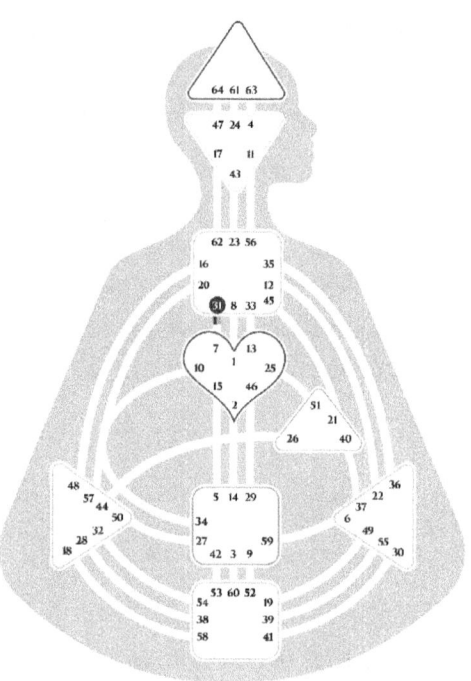

CHALLENGE:

To learn to lead as a representative of the people you are leading. To cultivate a leadership agenda of service. To not let your fear of not being seen, heard, or accepted get in the way of healthy leadership. To learn to take your rightful place as a leader and not hide out.

AFFIRMATION:

I am a natural born leader. I serve at my highest potential when I am empowering others by giving them a voice and then serving their needs. I use my power to lead people to a greater expansion of who they are and to support them in increasing their abundance, sustainability, and peace.

JOURNAL QUESTIONS:
- How do I feel about being a leader?
- Am I comfortable leading?
- Do I shrink from taking leadership?
- What is my place of service? Who do I serve?

EFT SETUP:
Even though I'm afraid to be seen, I now choose to express myself and the magnificence that is me with gusto, courage, and awareness of my own power and preciousness, and I deeply and completely love and accept myself.

EARTH:
Gate 41: Imagination

Your imagination is one of the most powerful creative tools you have access to. Spend time this week practicing using your imagination. What do you dream of? What other possibilities are there? Use your imagination to see other potential realities. You don't have to do what you imagine. Just use this power to stimulate creative emotional frequencies of energy.

JULY 29, 2026

FULL MOON

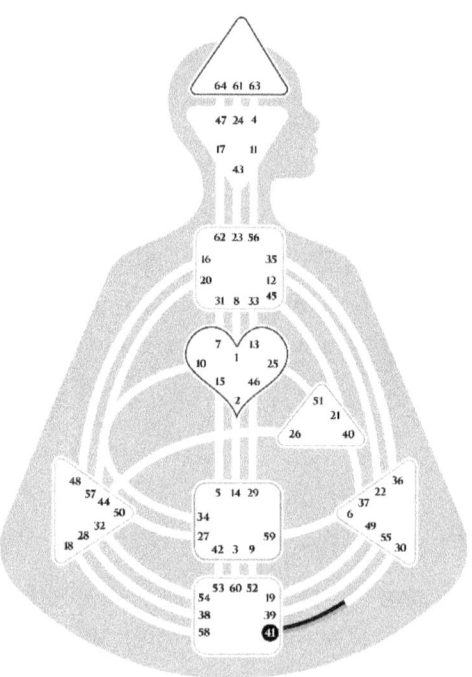

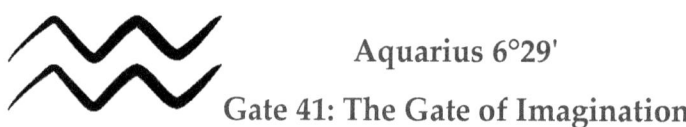

Aquarius 6°29'

Gate 41: The Gate of Imagination

Full moon energy invites us to explore what we need to release and let go of to stay in alignment with our intentions.

The light of the full moon on July 29, 2026, illuminates what must be healed, released, and aligned so we can move forward with clarity and power in our creative intentions. Full moons are potent opportunities to assess what's standing in the way of our expansion—and this particular full moon highlights Gate 41, the Gate of Imagination in Quantum Human Design. Gate 41 is the very starting point of the Human Design New Year, the seed from which all stories, all timelines, and all possibilities begin to unfold. It represents the beginning of everything: the moment before the story begins, the quiet spark of an idea before action takes form. This is the gate of divine dreaming.

Gate 41 reminds us that all creation begins first in the mind. What we imagine becomes the blueprint for what we manifest. This energy invites us to remember that imagination is not frivolous or unrealistic—it is the birthplace of innovation, transformation, and expansion. Your dreams matter. Your ability to dream and imagine is a sacred channel through which inspiration from the higher realms flows into form. It is the way we begin to vibrate with what's next, to attune our inner world with the direction our soul is calling us toward.

When we become disconnected from our imagination—when we stop dreaming or let our imagination become clouded by fear and limitation—we lose one of the most powerful tools in our creative toolbox. Instead of programming the mind to scan for hope and opportunity, we unconsciously instruct it to look for evidence of failure, danger, or restriction. This can result in feeling stuck, disillusioned, or uncertain about the future. Gate 41 calls us to cleanse the inner lens through which we dream, to lovingly weed out the distortions of fear, and to reinstate possibility as the primary lens through which we view the unfolding of our lives.

This full moon asks us to recommit to the sacred practice of dreaming. It is a reminder to imagine generously, to consciously use fantasy and visioning as tools for programming the brain and calibrating our energy field to what we desire. Our dreams are not just flights of fancy—they are instructions to the Universe and invitations to our higher self. Use this full moon to release the belief that imagination is impractical and instead honor it as one of your most essential creative superpowers. Dream big. Dream on purpose. And let your imagination become the luminous seed of the future you are here to bring to life.

CHALLENGE:

To optimize the energy of this full moon, you must learn to trust the power of your imagination as a sacred, creative force—not a distraction or indulgence. The lesson is to consciously direct your dreams toward expansion, hope, and possibility, knowing that what you imagine shapes the energy you emit and the opportunities you magnetize. When you take responsibility for the stories you tell yourself in your inner world, you begin to create a reality aligned with your highest creative potential.

OPTIMAL EXPRESSION:

The optimal expression of this full moon is a deep, embodied trust in your inner vision, where imagination becomes a channel for divine inspiration and a catalyst for aligned action. When you allow yourself to dream boldly and tend to those dreams with love and intention, you generate a frequency of possibility that calls in support, synchronicity, and creative flow. This full moon offers the experience of renewed faith in your role as a conscious creator, planting visionary seeds that shape the future.

UNBALANCED EXPRESSION:

The unbalanced experience of this full moon may show up as fear-based fantasizing, mental overwhelm, or a disconnection from your ability to dream and envision a hopeful future. You may feel stuck in limiting beliefs or unconsciously use your imagination to reinforce stories of lack, failure, or inevitability. Without conscious direction, this energy can distort your inner narrative and block the flow of creative momentum.

CONTEMPLATIONS:

- What dreams or inner visions quietly stirring within me have I dismissed as unrealistic or impractical?
- How am I currently using my imagination—am I feeding it with fear and limitation or with inspiration and expansion?
- What outdated beliefs or inner narratives need to be released for me to fully trust the power of my creative mind?
- In what ways can I consciously use imagination as a tool to calibrate my energy and prepare for aligned action?
- What would it feel like to make space for dreaming as a sacred, daily practice of devotion to my creative potential?

AFFIRMATION:

I honor the power of my imagination as a divine force of creation. I release fear and limitation, and I dream boldly, knowing that my visions are seeds of possibility. I trust the unfolding path and allow my inner world to shape a future aligned with inspiration, purpose, and joy.

JULY 31, 2026

GATE 33: RETELLING

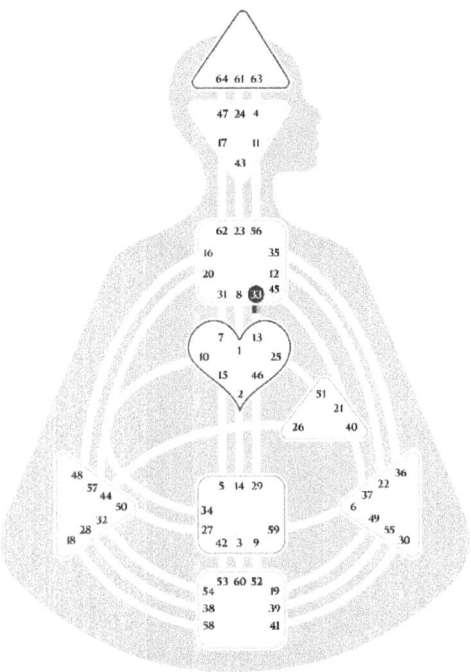

CHALLENGE:

To learn to share a personal narrative that reflects your true value and your worth. To share a personal narrative when it satisfies the intention to serve, improving the direction of others. To share history in an empowering way.

AFFIRMATION:

I am a processor of stories. My gift is my ability to help others find the blessings, the love, and the power from stories of pain. I hold people's secrets and stories and transform them to share when the time is right. The stories I tell change the direction of people's lives. I use the power of stories to increase the power of heart in the world and to help build a world of love.

JOURNAL QUESTIONS:

- What personal narratives am I telling that might be keeping me stuck, feeling like a victim, or feeling unlovable? How can I rewrite these stories?
- What listening practices do I have? What can I do to listen better so that I can gauge when it is the right time to share in a powerful way?

EFT SETUP:

Even though my stories from my past have held me back, I now choose to rewrite the story of my life and tell it the way I choose, with forgiveness, embracing the gifts and honoring my courage and strength in my story, and I deeply and completely love and accept myself.

EARTH:

Gate 19: Attunement

This week spend some time alone in nature. Notice how your energy feels in the restful embrace of the natural world. Practice feeling the energy of others and then contrasting it with your own energy so that you can better learn to distinguish your energy from the emotional energy around you.

AUGUST 6, 2026

GATE 7: COLLABORATION

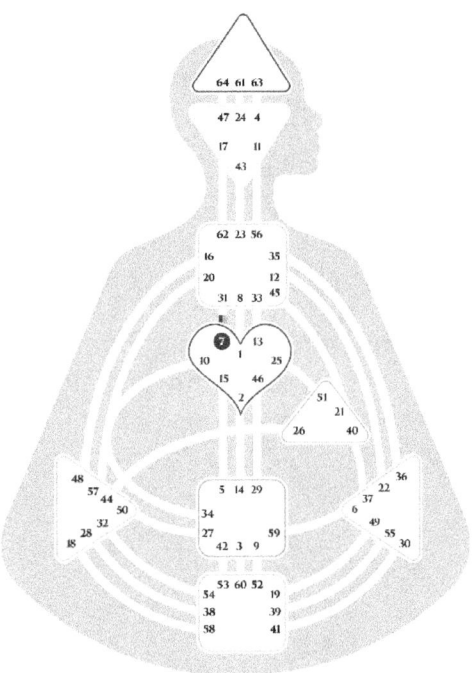

CHALLENGE:

To understand the need to be in front and allow yourself to serve through building teams, collaborating, and influencing the figurehead of leadership. To be at peace with serving the leader through support and collaboration. To recognize that the voice of the leader is only as strong and powerful as the support they receive.

AFFIRMATION:

I am an agent of peace who influences the direction and organization of leadership. I unify people around ideas. I influence with my wisdom, my knowledge, and my connections. I am a team builder and a collaborator, and I organize people in ways that empower and support them in creating a collective direction rooted in compassion.

JOURNAL QUESTIONS:

- What are my gifts and strengths? How do I use those gifts to influence and lead others?
- How do I feel about not being the figurehead of leadership?
- What happens when I only support the leadership? Do I still feel powerful? Influential?
- Make a list of the times when my influence has positively directed leadership.

EFT SETUP:

Even though I feel confused and conflicted about what to do, I trust the divine flow and let the Universe show me the right thing to do in the right time, and I deeply and completely love, trust, and accept myself.

EARTH:

Gate 13: Narrative

Take some time this week to really listen to the story you're telling about who you are. Is it big enough? Are you taking control of your own story or are you allowing the past to define who you are? If you were going to rewrite your story, what would you say about yourself? How can you make your personal narrative more true to who you really are?

AUGUST 12, 2026

NEW MOON AND TOTAL SOLAR ECLIPSE

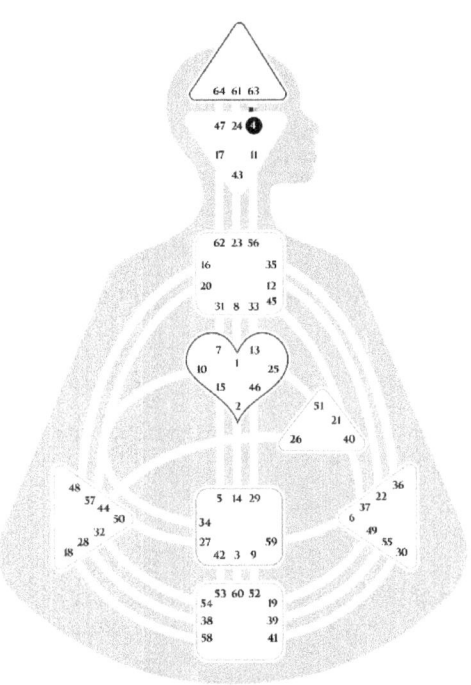

Leo 20°8'

Gate 4: The Gate of Possibility

The August 12, 2026, new moon and total solar eclipse is a profoundly potent moment of initiation. New moons always mark a time for setting intentions, planting seeds, and beginning anew—but when paired with a total solar eclipse, this energy is magnified exponentially. Eclipses accelerate change and often signify fated opportunities or course corrections. This is not an ordinary beginning. It's a powerful portal that invites us to courageously enter into a new cycle, even if we don't yet know exactly where we're going. The darkness of the eclipse holds the unknown, asking us to trust not in what we know but in what's possible.

This new moon eclipse shines its light on Gate 4 in Quantum Human Design—the Gate of Possibility. Gate 4 carries the pressure to find answers, to solve problems, and to make sense of things through logic and understanding. But this gate also holds a trap: the belief that we must have all the answers before we begin. When we can't find those answers, we often descend into doubt—especially self-doubt. That doubt can freeze us, keeping us from taking action on the dreams and visions we hold. It becomes easier to stay in familiar patterns, even when those patterns no longer serve us.

But this eclipse brings a different invitation. Rather than seeking certainty, we are asked to explore possibility. This is a time to begin a new experiment—one that may not come with guaranteed outcomes but that is necessary for growth. Possibility requires courage. It asks us to release outdated beliefs, habits, and structures that have kept us confined. The journey ahead is not about perfection or predictability. It's about allowing ourselves to try something new, even if we stumble along the way. From the quantum perspective, this is how new realities are born—through the boldness of not knowing and doing it anyway.

This eclipse is an activation. It asks us to rewire our relationship with doubt and to stop seeing it as a barrier but rather as a threshold into possibility. We are invited to build new internal and external infrastructures that support innovation, experimentation, and creative growth. We are not meant to walk into this next chapter with everything figured out. We are meant to walk forward with faith in the creative process itself—and in our ability to learn, adapt, and become more aligned as we go. This is a moon to embrace the unknown, release the need for certainty, and begin the worthy experiment of becoming something new.

CHALLENGE:

The greatest lesson of this new moon eclipse is that clarity is often born through action, not before it. We're being reminded that we don't need all the answers to begin—what we need is the courage to trust possibility and take the first step. This eclipse teaches us that doubt is not a stop sign but a signal that something new is ready to emerge through us.

OPTIMAL EXPRESSION:

The optimal expression of this new moon eclipse is a courageous willingness to explore new ideas without needing guaranteed outcomes. It's the embodiment of trust in the creative process, allowing possibility—not certainty—to lead the way. This energy supports building new patterns, structures, and rhythms that align with a higher, more liberated version of who we're becoming.

UNBALANCED EXPRESSION:

The unbalanced expression of this energy is becoming blocked by the need for certainty, allowing self-doubt to override intuition and inspiration. It can show up as overthinking, hesitating to start, or clinging to outdated structures out of fear of the unknown. In this state, the pressure to figure it out stifles creativity and keeps us trapped in cycles of inaction.

CONTEMPLATIONS:

- Where in my life am I waiting for certainty before I begin—and what might shift if I chose to begin anyway?
- What possibilities have I been quietly dreaming about that I'm now ready to explore more boldly?
- How has self-doubt kept me tethered to outdated systems, roles, or beliefs—and what am I ready to release?
- What new rhythms, habits, or structures could support the version of me that's ready to emerge?
- Am I willing to view this next chapter as a worthy experiment, even if I don't yet know where it will lead?

AFFIRMATION:

I trust in the power of possibility and give myself permission to begin, even without all the answers. I release doubt and step forward with courage, knowing that each step I take is shaping a new, aligned future.

AUGUST 12, 2026

GATE 4: POSSIBILITY

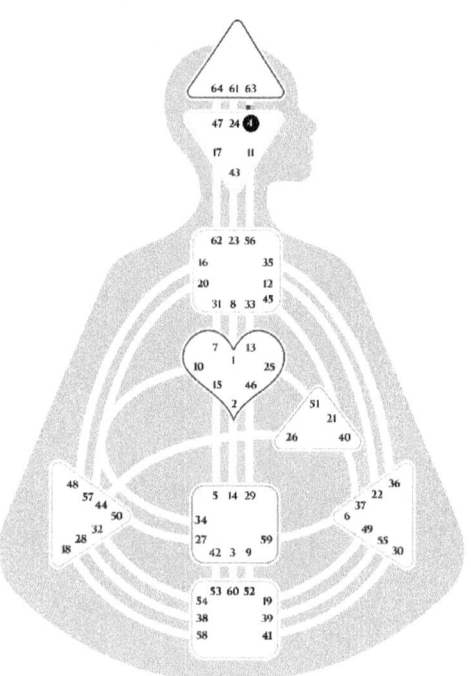

CHALLENGE:
To learn to embrace ideas as possibilities, not answers, and to let the power of the possibility stimulate the imagination as a way of calibrating the emotions and the heart. This gate teaches us the power of learning to wait to see which possibility actually manifests in the physical world and to experiment with options in response.

AFFIRMATION:
I am tuned into the cosmic flow of possibility. I am inspired about exploring new possibilities and potentials. I use the power of my thoughts to stretch the limits of what is known and engage my imagination to explore the potential of the unknown.

JOURNAL QUESTIONS:
- What ideas do I have right now that need me to nurture and activate them?
- What possibilities do these ideas stimulate right now? Take some time to write or visualize the possibilities.
- Am I comfortable with waiting? What can I do to increase my patience and curiosity?

EFT SETUP:
Even though I don't know what to do, I allow my questions to seed the Universe, and I trust and wait with great patience that the answers will be revealed to me, and I deeply and completely love and accept myself.

EARTH:
Gate 49: The Catalyst

Are you holding onto a situation for too long? Do you have a habit of quitting too soon? Is there a circumstance or condition in your life that you are allowing or running from because you fear the emotional energy associated with change? What needs to be healed or released?

AUGUST 17, 2026

GATE 29: DEVOTION

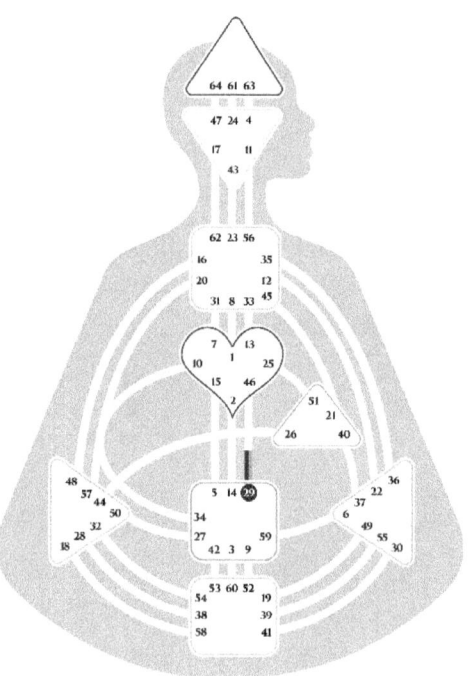

CHALLENGE:

To discover to what and to whom you need to devote yourself. To sustain yourself so that you can sustain your devotion. To learn to say no to what you need to say no to and to learn to say yes to what you want to say yes to.

AFFIRMATION:

I have an extraordinary ability to devote myself to the manifestation of an idea. My commitment to my story and to the fulfillment of my intention changes the story of what is possible in my own life and for humanity. I choose my commitments with great care. I devote myself to what is vital for the evolution of the world, and I nurture myself first because my well-being is the foundation of what I create.

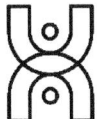
JOURNAL QUESTIONS:

- What devotion do I have right now that drives me?
- Is this a devotion that inspires me, or do I feel overly obligated to it?
- Who would I be and what would I choose if I gave myself permission to say no more often?
- What would I like to say no to that I am saying yes to right now?
- What obligations do I need to take off my plate right now?
- What would I like to devote myself to?

EFT SETUP:

Even though I am afraid to invest all my effort into my dream (What if it fails? What if I'm crazy? What if I just need to buckle down and be normal?), I now choose to do it anyway, and I deeply and completely love and accept myself.

EARTH:

Gate 30: Passion

What do you need to do this week to sustain your vision or dream about what you are inspired to create in your life?

AUGUST 23, 2026

GATE 59: SUSTAINABILITY

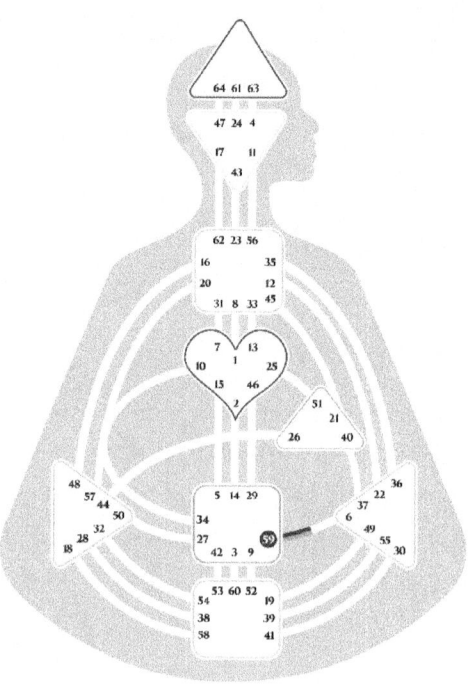

CHALLENGE:

To learn to make abundant choices that sustain you, and at the same time, others. To collaborate and initiate others into sustainable relationships from a place of sufficiency. To learn to share what you have in a sustainable way.

AFFIRMATION:

The energy that I carry has the power to create sufficiency and sustainability for all. I craft valuable alliances and agreements that support me in expanding abundance for everyone. I hold to higher principles and values that are rooted in my trust in sufficiency and the all-providing Source. Through my work and alignments my blessings serve to increase the blessings of myself and others.

JOURNAL QUESTIONS:

- Do I trust in my own abundance?
- How do I feel about sharing what I have with others?
- Am I creating relationship and partnership agreements that honor my work?
- Do I have relationships and agreements that are draining me? What needs to change?
- How do I feel about being right?
- Am I open to other ways of thinking or being?
- Do I believe in creating agreements and alignments with people who have different values and perspectives?

EFT SETUP:

Even though I struggle to share my intentions, I now choose to boldly state them and wait for the pieces of my creation to magically fall into place, and I deeply and completely love and accept myself.

EARTH:

Gate 55: Faith

This week deepen your experience of beauty. Surround yourself with beauty. Consciously bring beauty into your daily life and notice how abundantly beautiful life truly is.

AUGUST 28, 2026

FULL MOON AND PARTIAL LUNAR ECLIPSE

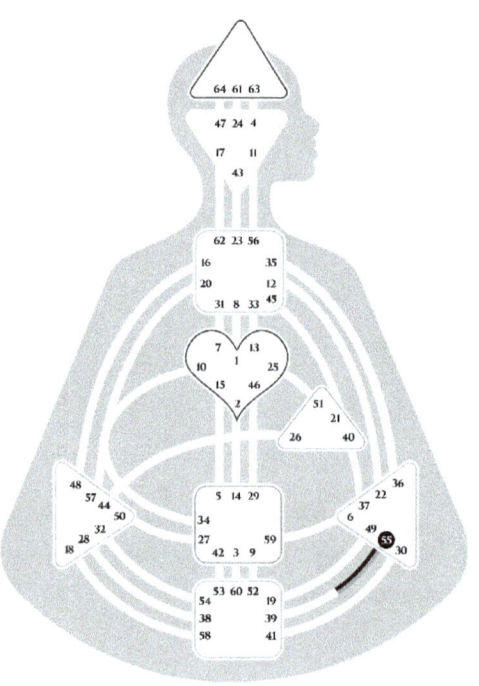

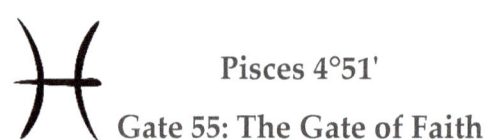

Pisces 4°51'

Gate 55: The Gate of Faith

Full moon energy invites us to explore what we need to release and let go of to stay in alignment with our intentions. Eclipse energy amplifies the intensity of the full moon.

The full moon on August 28, 2026, is a partial lunar eclipse that illuminates Gate 55, the Gate of Faith in Quantum Human Design. As with every full moon, we are invited to examine what needs to be released so that we can continue to align with our authentic intentions. But eclipses add intensity, acting as catalytic turning points that accelerate our growth. This eclipse brings a heightened invitation to let go of what undermines our faith, particularly the fear, doubt, and control patterns that keep us clinging to certainty and linear logic. The light of this moon shines on our relationship with trust, asking us to relinquish the need to know every detail before we take action.

Gate 55 is an emotional gate—one that oscillates between abundance and emptiness, between deep longing and ecstatic possibility. It is where our emotional energy becomes the fertile ground for manifestation—but only if we trust the cycles and allow ourselves to be resourced by something greater than our limited human will. This eclipse reminds us that real faith isn't passive. It's not about waiting for proof. It's about surrendering into the mystery with open hands and open hearts, willing to receive without demanding guarantees. We are asked to release our attachment to rigid expectations, timelines, or step-by-step certainty and instead rest in the deep knowing that we are held.

This full moon also builds on the energetic momentum seeded during the August 12 new moon total solar eclipse in Gate 4, the Gate of Possibility. That new moon challenged us to begin—even without all the answers—and to step into new territory guided by curiosity rather than certainty. Now, this lunar eclipse asks us to let go of the fear that we'll be unsupported in the process. It asks us to deepen our faith in the unfolding path, in divine timing, and in our own worthiness. We are being recalibrated for bigger dreams, but to receive the next right step, we have to release the grip of self-doubt and reclaim our trust in the unseen architecture of life.

Ultimately, the eclipse in Gate 55 reminds us that faith is a frequency. When we align with it, we magnetize the people, resources, and synchronicities that are aligned with our soul's blueprint. This full moon is not only a time to clear out what blocks our trust—it's also a powerful opportunity to declare that we are ready to build something bold, beautiful, and aligned with our divine enoughness. Faith is not only believing in what is possible—it's believing that you are the one who is meant to bring it to life.

CHALLENGE:

The lesson of this full moon lunar eclipse is to deepen our trust in the unseen and to release the fear that we must have it all figured out before we begin. It teaches us that true faith means aligning with our worthiness to be supported by the Universe and surrendering control so that the next right step can be revealed. This moon reminds us that we are not meant to build alone—we are meant to cocreate with the infinite.

OPTIMAL EXPRESSION:

The optimal expression of this full moon energy is a deep, embodied trust in the flow of life and an unwavering belief in our divine support. It is the willingness to release control, take inspired action, and allow our faith to magnetize aligned opportunities and resources. When we fully align with this frequency, we become powerful cocreators of a vision greater than what we could build on our own.

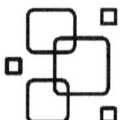
UNBALANCED EXPRESSION:

In its unbalanced expression, this full moon may stir up fear, doubt, and emotional volatility—especially around not knowing what's next or feeling unsupported. It can trigger a need to control outcomes, cling to old plans, or fall into hopelessness and lack when the path ahead feels unclear. Instead of leaning into trust, we may try to force certainty, which only amplifies resistance and disconnects us from the intuitive guidance available to us.

CONTEMPLATIONS:

- What beliefs or stories am I holding onto that block me from fully trusting the process of my life?
- Where in my life am I trying to force clarity or control, rather than allowing space for divine timing to unfold?
- How can I deepen my connection to a greater source of support—both within myself and beyond myself?
- What would it feel like to move forward without having all the answers but with full faith that I will be guided?
- In what ways am I being invited to dream bigger—and do I believe I am worthy of receiving what I truly desire?

AFFIRMATION:

I trust the unfolding of my life, even when the path is unclear. I release the need for certainty and open myself to divine support, knowing that I am worthy of building something greater than I can imagine.

AUGUST 29, 2026

GATE 40: RESTORATION

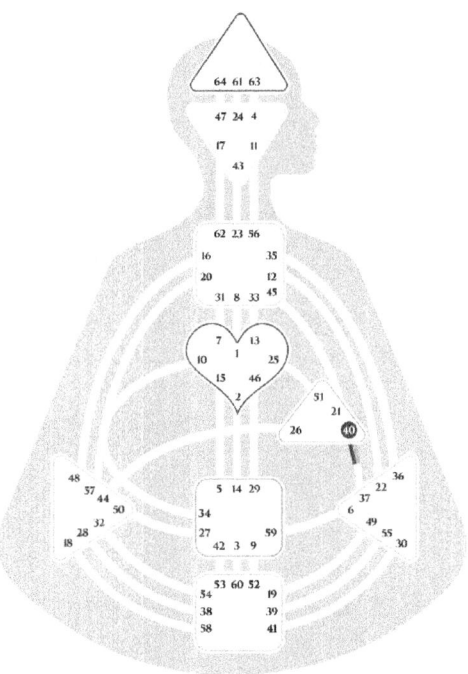

CHALLENGE:

To learn to value yourself enough to retreat from community and the energy of those you love to restore, restock, and replenish your inner resources. To learn to interpret the signal of loneliness correctly. To take responsibility for your own care and resources and to not abdicate your own power to take care of yourself.

AFFIRMATION:

I am a powerful resource for my community. The energy that I hold impacts others deeply and brings them to deeper states of alignment and sustainability. I take care of my body, mind, and soul because I know the more that I am and the more that I have, the more I can give to others. I take care of myself first because I know that good things flow from me. I am valuable and powerful, and I claim and defend the true story of who I am.

JOURNAL QUESTIONS:

- What role does loneliness play in my life?
- Has loneliness caused me to doubt my value?
- What do I need to do to restore my energy?
- Am I doing enough to take care of myself?
- What agreements am I making in my relationships that might be causing me to compromise my value?
- How can I rewrite these agreements?
- Am I abdicating my responsibility for my self-care?
- Am I living a martyr model?
- What needs to be healed, released, aligned, and brought to my awareness for me to take responsibility for cultivating my own sense of value and my self-worth?

EFT SETUP:

Even though it is hard to let go of the obligations of relationships, I now choose to release all relationships that are draining and unsupportive, and I deeply and completely love and accept myself.

EARTH:

Gate 37: Peace

When you feel that your outer world is chaotic and disrupted, how do you cultivate inner peace? Practice anchoring yourself in deep inner peace this week.

SEPTEMBER 4, 2026

GATE 64: DIVINE TRANSFERENCE

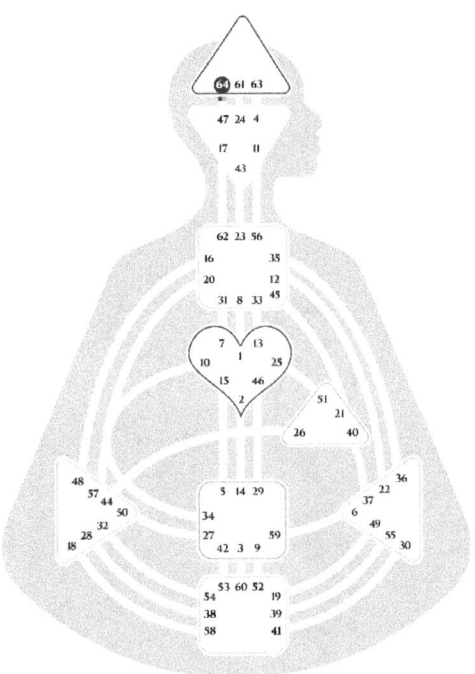

CHALLENGE:

To not let the power of your big ideas overwhelm you and shut down your dreaming and creating. To not get lost in the pressure of answering the how question.

AFFIRMATION:

I am a conduit for expansive thinking. My inspirations and ideas create the seeds of possibility in my mind and in the mind of others. I honor the dreams that pass through my mind and allow my big ideas to stimulate my imagination and the imagination of others. I trust the Universe to reveal the details of my dreams when the time is right. I use the power of my dreams to stimulate a world of possibility and expansion.

JOURNAL QUESTIONS:
- What do I do to take care of my big ideas?
- How do I feel about having dreams but not always the solutions?
- How can I stop judging the gift of my dreams?
- Do I trust that the how of my ideas will be revealed?
- How can I deepen this trust?

EFT SETUP:
Even though I don't know what is next, I wait and trust that the perfect right step will show up for me, and I deeply and completely love and accept myself. Even though I feel overwhelmed with ideas, I trust the Universe to reveal the next step to me. I relax and wait, and I deeply and completely love and accept myself.

EARTH:
Gate 63: Curiosity

What needs to happen to unlock your attachment to being right and to allow yourself to dream of other possibilities? What if there's more than what you can see right now?

SEPTEMBER 10, 2026

GATE 47: MINDSET

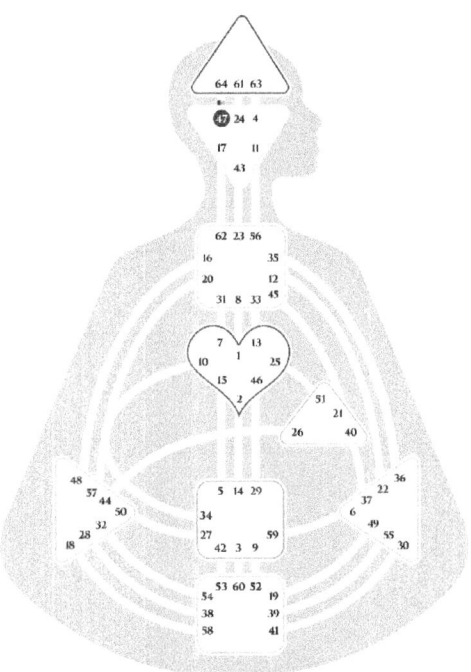

CHALLENGE:

To become skilled at a mindset of openness and possibility. To not let inspiration die because you don't know how to fulfill it.

AFFIRMATION:

My mindset is the source of my inspired actions and attitude. I know that when I receive an idea and inspiration, it is my job to nurture the idea by using the power of my imagination to increase the potential and emotional frequency of the idea. I consistently keep my inner and outer environment aligned with the energy of possibility and potential. I know that it is my job to create by virtue of my alignment, and I relax knowing that it is the job of the Universe to fulfill my inspirations.

JOURNAL QUESTIONS:

- What thoughts do I have when I receive an idea or inspiration?
- Am I hopeful or despairing?
- How does it feel to let go of figuring out how I'm going to make my idea a reality?
- What do I do to regulate my mindset?
- What practices do I need to cultivate to increase the power of my thoughts?

EFT SETUP:

Even though it is frustrating to not know how to make something happen, I now choose to wait for divine insight, and I trust that the right information will be revealed to me at the perfect time, and I deeply and completely love and accept myself.

EARTH:

Gate 22: Surrender

Where are you denying your passion in your life? What is one thing you can do this week to reclaim your passion?

SEPTEMBER 11, 2026

NEW MOON

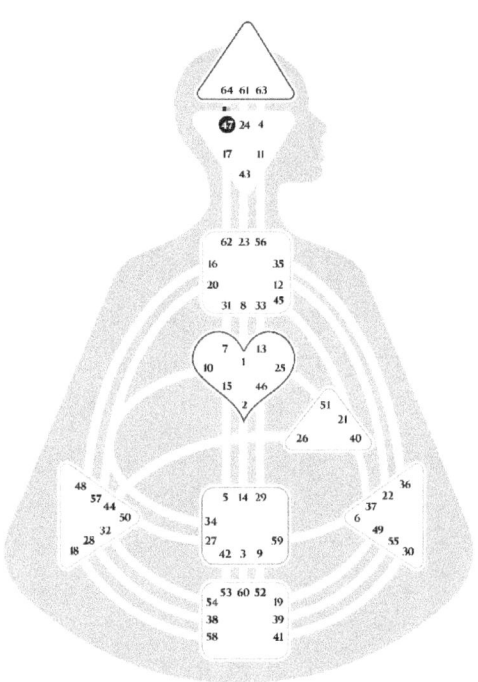

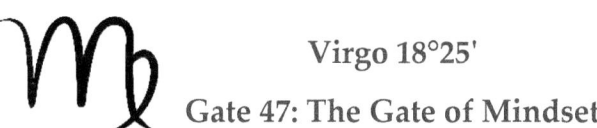

Virgo 18°25'

Gate 47: The Gate of Mindset

New moon energy invites us to explore how we can deepen our alignment with our intentions and asks us to focus on what we want to grow and expand on in our lives.

The new moon on September 11, 2026, invites us into a sacred pause—an opportunity to recalibrate, reset, and plant new seeds of intention. As with all new moons, this is a time of beginnings—a moment to turn inward, listen deeply, and align with the subtle whispers of our next becoming. When we honor the quiet, generative power of the new moon, we create space for dreams to emerge, visions to take root, and new directions to reveal themselves. This moon in particular brings us into communion with the energy of Gate 47, the Gate of Mindset in Quantum Human Design.

Gate 47 teaches us that we do not have to see the entire path before we begin. This energy encourages us to take the next right step and then the next, building momentum through trust, alignment, and faithful action. So often we delay our becoming because we believe we must have it all figured out in advance. But true innovation and expansion come from a mindset that allows for mystery—a mindset that makes space for grace, trust, and divine timing. We are reminded that manifestation doesn't begin with certainty. It begins with vision, willingness, and belief.

Our mindset is not simply a mental state—it is an energetic frequency. The stories we tell ourselves shape the hormones we produce, the thoughts we believe, and even the way we regulate our emotions and biology. A healthy, aligned mindset opens the door to heart coherence and higher-order thinking. But in the shadow expression of this gate, we shrink from our big dreams when we don't yet see how they can come to pass. We fear we don't have enough answers or that we aren't ready—and so we delay, minimize, or abandon what wants to grow through us.

This new moon is a potent invitation to shift the stories we're telling. What if not knowing how was not a reason to stop—but an opening for greater creativity? What if we no longer made "not yet" mean "not possible"? This moon calls us to recommit to the power of mindset as an instrument of manifestation. We are asked to dream boldly, to speak life into possibility, and to steward our ideas not with perfectionism but with presence, devotion, and faith. Let this be a time to think big, to trust the unfolding, and to remember that the most powerful thing we can plant in the dark fertile soil of a new moon… is belief.

CHALLENGE:

This new moon teaches us that clarity is born through movement, not certainty. It reminds us that our mindset shapes the reality we're capable of creating—and that belief must come before evidence. Most importantly, it calls us to stop waiting for the perfect plan and start trusting the power of the next aligned step.

OPTIMAL EXPRESSION:

The optimal expression of this moon is a mindset rooted in trust, expansion, and possibility. It is the willingness to dream beyond what feels logical, to stay devoted to vision even in uncertainty, and to take inspired action without needing the full map. From this place, manifestation becomes a natural extension of aligned thought, belief, and courage.

UNBALANCED EXPRESSION:

The unbalanced expression of this moon energy can show up as mental overwhelm, confusion, or the tendency to overanalyze instead of act. When we feel pressured to have it all figured out, we may downsize our dreams, abandon our ideas, or delay movement out of fear. This can keep us stuck in stories of limitation, disconnected from the deeper wisdom that guides us step by step.

CONTEMPLATIONS:
- What dream or idea have I been postponing because I don't yet know how it will unfold?
- Where am I being invited to take the next right step, even without a full plan?
- What stories am I telling myself that limit what's possible for me?
- How can I shift my mindset to one of trust, expansion, and aligned possibility?
- What does it feel like in my body when I choose belief over fear?

AFFIRMATION:

I trust the unfolding of my path. I don't need to know every step—I only need the courage to take the next one. My mind is a powerful vessel for vision, and I choose to believe in what's possible.

SEPTEMBER 15, 2026

GATE 6: IMPACT

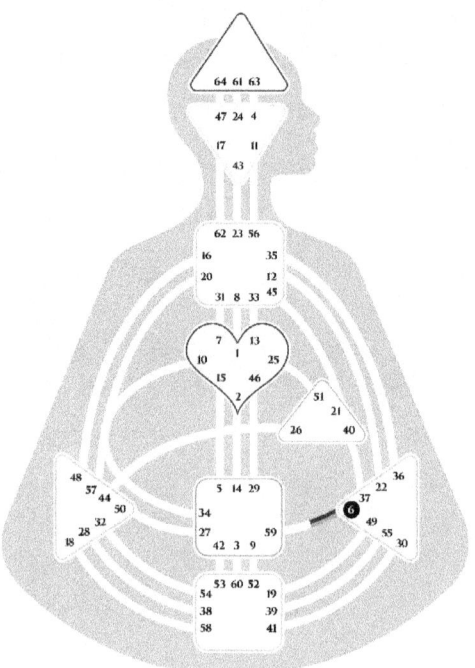

CHALLENGE:

To become proficient in using emotional energy and learn to trust that your impact is in service to the world. When you understand that your life is a vehicle for service and your energy is being used to influence and impact those around you, you assume greater obligation and responsibility to maintain a high frequency of energy. The quality of the emotional energy you cultivate influences others to come together in an equitable, sustainable, and peaceful way. Learning to trust that your words and impact will have effect when the timing is correct and not overriding divine timing.

AFFIRMATION:

My emotional energy influences the world around me. I am rooted in the energy of equity, sustainability, and peace. When I am aligned with abundance, I am an energetic source of influence that facilitates elegant solutions to creating peace and well-being. I am deliberate and aligned with values that create peace in my life, in my community, and in the world.

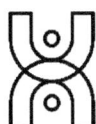

JOURNAL QUESTIONS:
- What do I need to do to deepen my trust in divine timing?
- What do I need to do to prepare myself to be seen and to have influence?
- What do I need to do to sustain my emotional energy in order to align with peaceful and sustainable solutions?
- How do I feel about lack? How do I feel about abundance? How can I create a greater degree of emotional abundance in my life? In my daily practice?

EFT SETUP:
Even though I am ready to leap into action, I now choose to take a breath, wait out my emotions, and trust that the right timing will be revealed to me. I'm not missing out on anything. Divine order is the rule of the day, and I deeply and completely love and accept myself.

EARTH:
Gate 36: Exploration

Go on a miracle hunt today. Make a list of all the unexpected synchronous and serendipitous events that have happened in your life. What has been the greatest miracle or unexpected event you've experienced in your life?

SEPTEMBER 21, 2026

GATE 46: EMBODIMENT

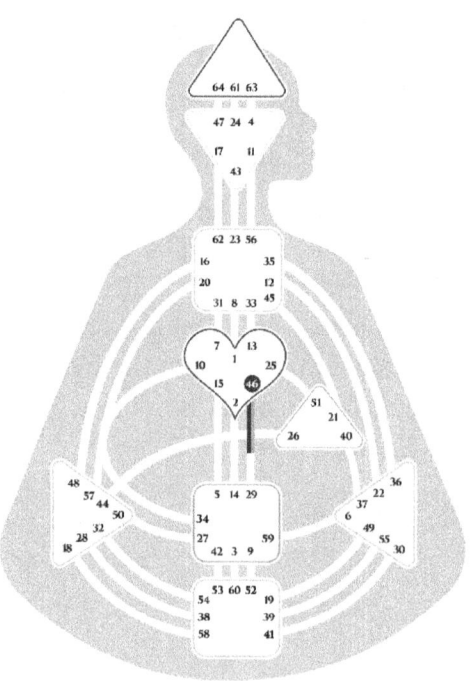

CHALLENGE:

To learn to love your body. To learn to fully be in your body. To learn to love the sensual nature of your physical form and to move it with love and awareness.

AFFIRMATION:

My body is the vehicle for my soul. My ability to fully express who I am (and my life and soul purpose) is deeply rooted in my body's ability to carry my soul. I love, nurture, and commit to my body. I appreciate all of its miraculous abilities and form. Every day, I love my body more.

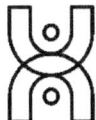
JOURNAL QUESTIONS:
- Do I love my body?
- What can I do to deepen my love for my body?
- What parts of my body do I love and appreciate?
- Make a list of every part of my body that I love.
- What do I need to do to amplify the life force I am experiencing in my body?
- What kinds of devotion and commitment do I experience that help me harness greater amounts of life force in my body?
- How can I deepen my commitment and devotion to my body?

EFT SETUP:
Even though it is hard for me to love my body, I now choose to embrace my amazing physical form and honor it for all the good it brings me, and I deeply and completely love and accept myself.

EARTH:
Gate 25: Spirit

Do you have a regular practice that connects you to Source? How can you deepen this practice this week?

SEPTEMBER 26, 2026

FULL MOON

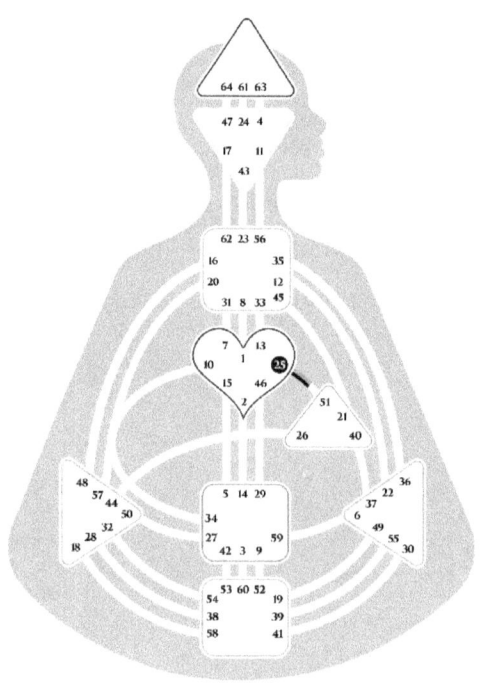

Aries 3°36'

Gate 25: The Gate of Spirit

Full moon energy invites us to explore what we need to release and let go of to stay in alignment with our intentions.

The full moon on September 26, 2026, brings with it a powerful moment of illumination and release. Full moon energy is always an invitation to let go—to surrender anything that no longer aligns with who we are becoming. It shines a light on what must be healed in order for us to grow into the next version of ourselves. This particular full moon reflects back to us the intentions we seeded during the new moon earlier this month, when we were encouraged to embrace a new mindset and begin, even in the absence of certainty or a complete plan.

Now, the light of the moon turns inward, calling us to examine the beliefs that may be preventing us from fully trusting in divine support. Are we clinging to fears that we have to do it all on our own? Are we burdened by the illusion that we must earn our worthiness before we can be held, guided, or resourced by something greater than ourselves? This moon asks us to release the scarcity stories that limit our capacity to receive—to finally let go of the need to control every outcome and instead surrender to the infinite wellspring of divine provision.

The second invitation of this moon is to reconnect with our higher purpose—not just as a concept, but as a living, breathing presence in our lives. It asks us to remember that we are each here to serve a unique and essential role in the unfolding of the cosmic story. When we forget the value of our contribution, we may hesitate, shrink, or delay taking action. But this moon urges us to reclaim the truth: Our life's purpose is significant, and our willingness to honor it is what activates the flow of faith, energy, and support we need to move forward.

In essence, this full moon is a mirror—reflecting back the questions our soul most needs to answer. Do we trust that we are not alone? Do we believe that our purpose matters? And are we willing to release the doubts that keep us from receiving the full backing of the Universe? Let this be a moment of remembering, of surrender, and of realignment with the sacred truth of your value and your place in the greater plan.

CHALLENGE:

The big lesson of this full moon is about surrendering the illusion of separation and stepping into radical trust—trust that we are fully supported by the Universe and that our higher purpose is both worthy and necessary. It challenges us to release the doubts that keep us small and to remember that our alignment with purpose is what activates the flow of divine guidance, resources, and support.

OPTIMAL EXPRESSION:

The optimal expression of this full moon is a deep, embodied trust in both divine support and the significance of our higher purpose. It looks like courageous action rooted in faith, a willingness to let go of control, and an openhearted alignment with the truth that our lives are valuable manifestations of a greater cosmic plan.

UNBALANCED EXPRESSION:

The unbalanced expression of this full moon shows up as fear-driven control, self-doubt, and a disconnection from divine support. It can manifest as clinging to old stories of unworthiness, hesitation to step into purpose, or believing we must do everything alone. This energy may feel heavy, anxious, or uncertain when we resist surrender.

CONTEMPLATIONS:

- What am I still holding onto that keeps me from fully trusting in the support of God, Source, or the Universe?
- In what areas of my life am I trying to control the outcome instead of surrendering to divine timing and flow?
- Do I believe that my higher purpose is valuable and worthy of full support—and if not, what stories are blocking that belief?
- How might I live, speak, or create differently if I truly trusted that I am here on purpose, for a purpose?
- What would it look like to release the weight of self-doubt and move forward in faith, even without all the answers?

AFFIRMATION:

I trust that I am fully supported by the Universe. My life is a sacred expression of a higher purpose, and I am worthy of all the guidance, resources, and love I need to fulfill it.

SEPTEMBER 27, 2026

GATE 18: RE-ALIGNMENT

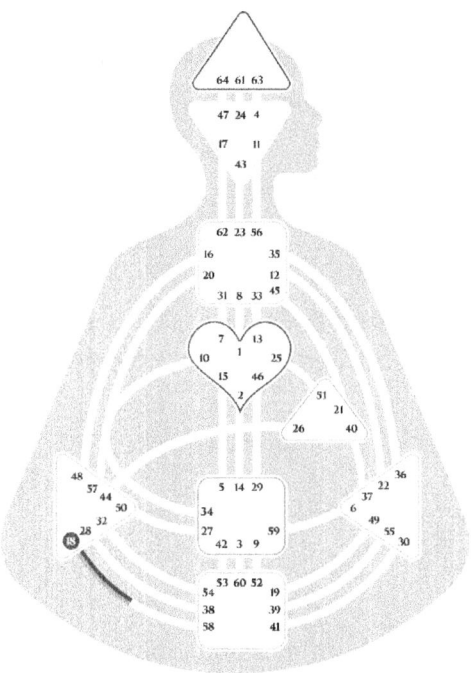

CHALLENGE:

To learn to wait for the right timing and the right circumstances to offer your intuitive insights into how to fix or correct a pattern. To wait for the right time and the right reason to share your critique. To understand that the purpose of realignment is to create more joy, not to be "right."

AFFIRMATION:

I am a powerful force that realigns patterns. My insights and awareness give people the information they need to deepen their expertise and to experience greater joy. I serve joy, and I align the patterns of the world to increase the world's potential for living in the flow of joy.

JOURNAL QUESTIONS:

- What does joy mean to me? How do I serve it? How do I cultivate joy in my own life?
- How does it feel to be right about something and keep it to myself?
- Do I need to release any old stories about needing to be right?
- Do I trust my own insights? Do I have the courage to share them when it is necessary?

EFT SETUP:

Even though I feel criticized and judged, I now choose to hear the wisdom of the correction and release my personal attachment, and I deeply and completely love and accept myself.

EARTH:

Gate 17: Anticipation

What do you need to do to release any doubts and fears you may have about your own ability? What accomplishments do you have that you can celebrate and acknowledge?

OCTOBER 3, 2026

GATE 48: WISDOM

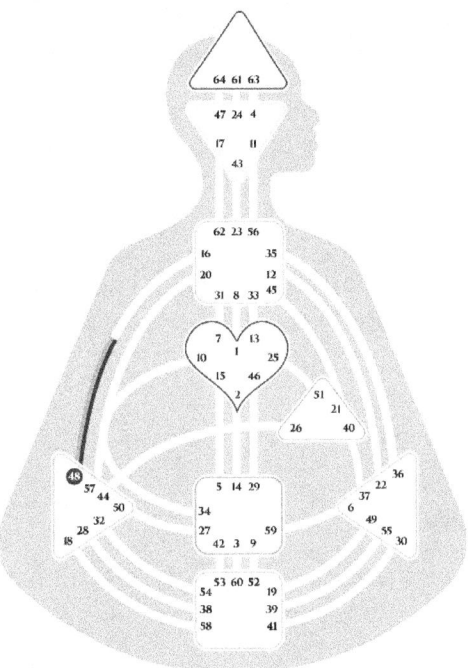

CHALLENGE:

To allow yourself to trust that you will know what you need to know when you need to know it. To not let the fear of not knowing stop you from creating. To not let not knowing hold you back.

AFFIRMATION:

I am a depth of wisdom and knowledge. My studies and experiences have taught me everything I need to know. I push beyond the limits of my earthly knowledge and take great leaps of faith as a function of my deep connection to Source, knowing that I will always know what I need to know when I need to know it.

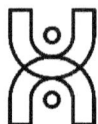
JOURNAL QUESTIONS:
- Do I trust my own knowing?
- What needs to be healed, released, aligned, and brought to my awareness for me to deepen my self-trust?
- What practice do I have that keeps me connected to the wisdom of Source?
- How can I deepen my connection to Source?

EFT SETUP:
Even though I am afraid I am not ready to, I now choose to courageously dive in and just do it, and I deeply and completely love and accept myself.

EARTH:
Gate 21: Self-Regulation

How can you be more generous with yourself this week? How can you create an inner and outer environment that is more self-generous?

OCTOBER 8, 2026

GATE 57: INSTINCT

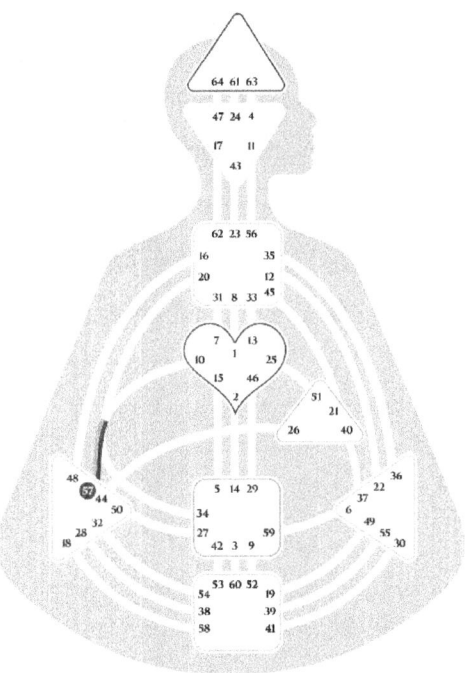

CHALLENGE:

To learn to trust your own insights and gut. To learn to tell the difference between an instinctive response versus a fear of the future. To become skilled at your connection to your sense of right timing.

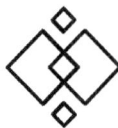

AFFIRMATION:

My inner wisdom is deeply connected to the pulse of divine timing. I listen to my inner wisdom and follow my instinct. I know when and how to prepare the way for the future. I take guided action, and I trust myself and Source.

JOURNAL QUESTIONS:
- Do I trust my intuition?
- What does my intuition feel like to me?
- Sometimes doing a retrospective analysis of my intuition or instinct makes it more clear how my intuitive signal works. What experiences in the past have I had where I knew I should or shouldn't have done something?
- How have I experienced my intuition in the past?
- When I think about moving forward in my life, do I feel afraid?
- What am I afraid of? What can I do to mitigate the fear?
- What impulses am I experiencing that are telling me to prepare for what is next in my life?
- Am I acting on my impulses? Why or why not?

EFT SETUP:
Even though it is scary to trust my gut, I now choose to honor my awareness, quiet my mind, and go with what feels right, and I deeply and completely love and accept myself.

EARTH:
Gate 51: Initiation

What lessons have unexpected events brought into your life? Make note of how resilient you are…

OCTOBER 10, 2026

NEW MOON

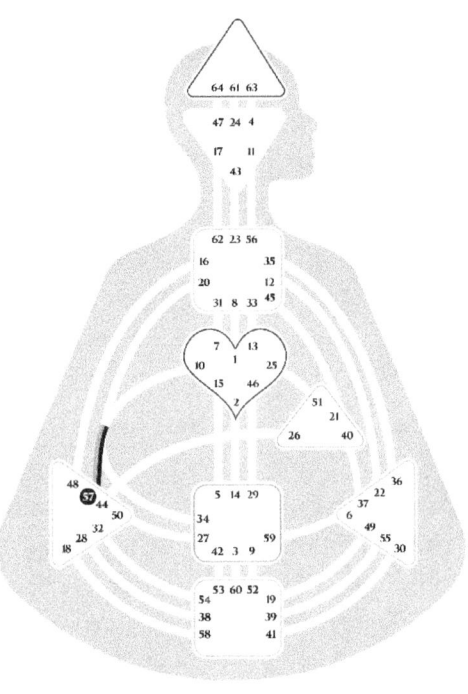

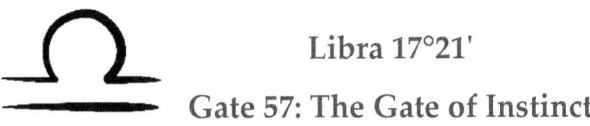

Libra 17°21'

Gate 57: The Gate of Instinct

New moon energy invites us to explore how we can deepen our alignment with our intentions and asks us to focus on what we want to grow and expand on in our lives.

The October 10, 2026, new moon invites us to begin a new season of intuitive alignment and deeper self-trust. New moons mark the initiation of new cycles, and this particular lunation—highlighting Gate 57, the Gate of Instinct in Quantum Human Design—calls us inward, toward the quiet wisdom that lives in the present moment. It reminds us that we are designed to navigate life not solely with logic but with the subtle inner signals that rise up from deep within. This is an initiation into learning how to listen to your instincts without needing external validation.

Gate 57 carries a frequency of profound intuitive awareness, a kind of knowing that arises instantaneously, often without explanation. This knowing is deeply accurate, but not always easy to trust—especially in a world that conditions us to value logic, evidence, and proof. Under this new moon, we are asked to explore what it means to act on our inner knowing even when it defies convention or predictability. What if the only plan we need is to stay attuned to the next right step that reveals itself through instinct?

In the shadow, Gate 57 can trigger fear—especially fear of the future. This fear can freeze us, keeping us stuck in outdated situations or holding patterns because the unknown feels too risky. But the gift of this energy is not to eliminate fear but to soften its grip by strengthening trust. This new moon shines a light on the ways we've learned to second-guess ourselves, defer to outside authority, or wait for circumstances to become "safe" before taking action. It is a time to consciously release those patterns.

This moon is not about having all the answers—it's about practicing courage in the absence of certainty. It asks us to attune more closely to the voice within, to honor our inner wisdom even when it doesn't make sense on paper. The beginning we are being called to make is one rooted in radical self-trust. When we move from this place, we are no longer reacting to fear, but responding to a deeper, divine intelligence that knows exactly where we're going—even if we don't.

CHALLENGE:

This moon teaches that true guidance doesn't always come with logic, certainty, or proof. It arises as instinct, intuition, a quiet knowing that often defies explanation. The challenge—and the gift—of this new moon is to stop outsourcing your clarity and start honoring the wisdom that lives within you. To move forward, you must release the fear of the future and the need for external validation and instead root yourself in the present moment, where your inner compass is already pointing you in the right direction. The future belongs to those brave enough to follow what they know, not just what they can explain.

OPTIMAL EXPRESSION:

The optimal expression of the October 10, 2026, new moon is fearless alignment with your inner truth. When this energy is expressed at its highest frequency, it looks like clear, embodied trust in your own instincts—even when the path ahead is uncertain. It's the quiet power of acting on what you feel to be right without needing to justify it. You are deeply present, attuned to subtle signals, and able to respond with clarity and grace rather than react from fear. You move through the world with a calm confidence, grounded not in what's predictable but in what's true for you in each moment. In this optimal state, your intuition becomes a sacred ally, guiding you to make bold, aligned decisions that shape a future you can't yet see— but are already becoming.

UNBALANCED EXPRESSION:

The unbalanced experience of this new moon may show up as stifling fear, self-doubt, and an overreliance on logic or outside opinions. You may feel stuck, unable to move forward because you don't know for sure, even though your intuition is quietly urging you onward. This can create a loop of hesitation, anxiety, and mistrust in your own inner wisdom.

CONTEMPLATIONS:

- Where in my life am I waiting for external proof or permission instead of trusting what I already know?
- What does my intuition feel like in my body—and how can I learn to recognize it more clearly?
- What fears about the future are keeping me from taking the next aligned step?
- What would it look like to honor my inner knowing, even if it doesn't make logical sense?
- What can I release—thoughts, habits, relationships, or beliefs—that blocks me from fully trusting myself?

AFFIRMATION:

I trust my inner knowing. I move forward with courage, even when the path is unclear. My intuition is wise, timely, and always guiding me home to myself.

OCTOBER 14, 2026

GATE 32: ENDURANCE

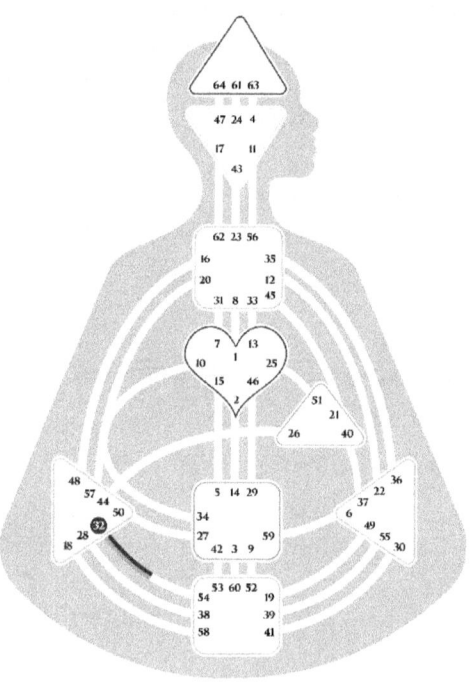

CHALLENGE:

To trust in divine timing. To prepare for the next step of manifestation and to align with the unfolding of the process. To be patient.

AFFIRMATION:

I am a divine translator for divine inspiration. I sense and know what needs to be prepared on the earthly plane in order to be ready for right timing. I am aligned with right timing, and I prepare and wait patiently, knowing that when the time is right, I am ready to do the work to help transform pain into power.

JOURNAL QUESTIONS:
- What do I need to do to be prepared to manifest my vision?
- What actionable steps need to be completed for me to be ready when the timing is right?
- What do I need to do to cultivate patience?
- Do I have a fear of failing that is causing me to avoid being prepared?
- Am I overdoing and being overly prepared?
- Am I pushing too hard?
- What can I let go of?

EFT SETUP:
Even though I have worked hard to make my dreams come true and nothing has happened yet, I trust in divine timing and keep tending to my vision, and I deeply and completely love and accept myself.

EARTH:
Gate 42: Conclusion

To get the most of this week, explore what unfinished business you need to bring to a conclusion. Are there things you need to say? Situations you need to end and be done with? Endings make room for new beginnings…

OCTOBER 20, 2026

GATE 50: NURTURING

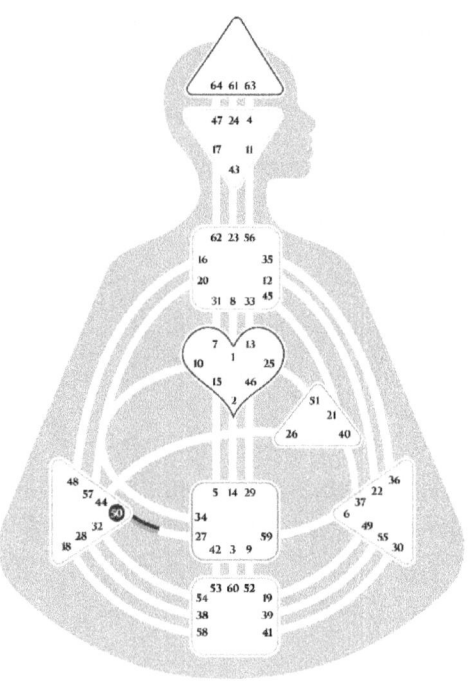

CHALLENGE:

To transcend guilt and unhealthy obligation and do what you need to do to take care of yourself in order to better serve others. To not hold to rigid principles to judge others.

AFFIRMATION:

My presence brings love into the room. I nurture and love others. I take care of myself first in order to be better able to serve love. I intuitively know what people need, and I facilitate for them a state of self-love and self-empowerment by helping them align more deeply with the power of love. I let go, and I allow others to learn from what I model and teach. I am a deep well of love that sustains the planet.

JOURNAL QUESTIONS:

- How do I feel about taking care of myself first?
- How do I sustain my nurturing energy?
- What role does guilt play in driving and/or motivating me?
- What would I choose if I could remove the guilt?
- Do I have nonnegotiable values? What are they?
- How do I handle people who share different values from me?

EFT SETUP:

Even though it is hard for me to give and receive love, I now choose to be completely open to receiving and sharing deep and unconditional love, starting by deeply and completely loving and accepting myself first.

EARTH:

Gate 3: Innovation

What is working in your life? Take some time to contemplate what aspects of your current reality you'd love to grow and expand upon.

OCTOBER 24, 2026–NOVEMBER 13, 2026

MERCURY RETROGRADE

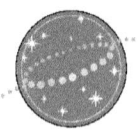

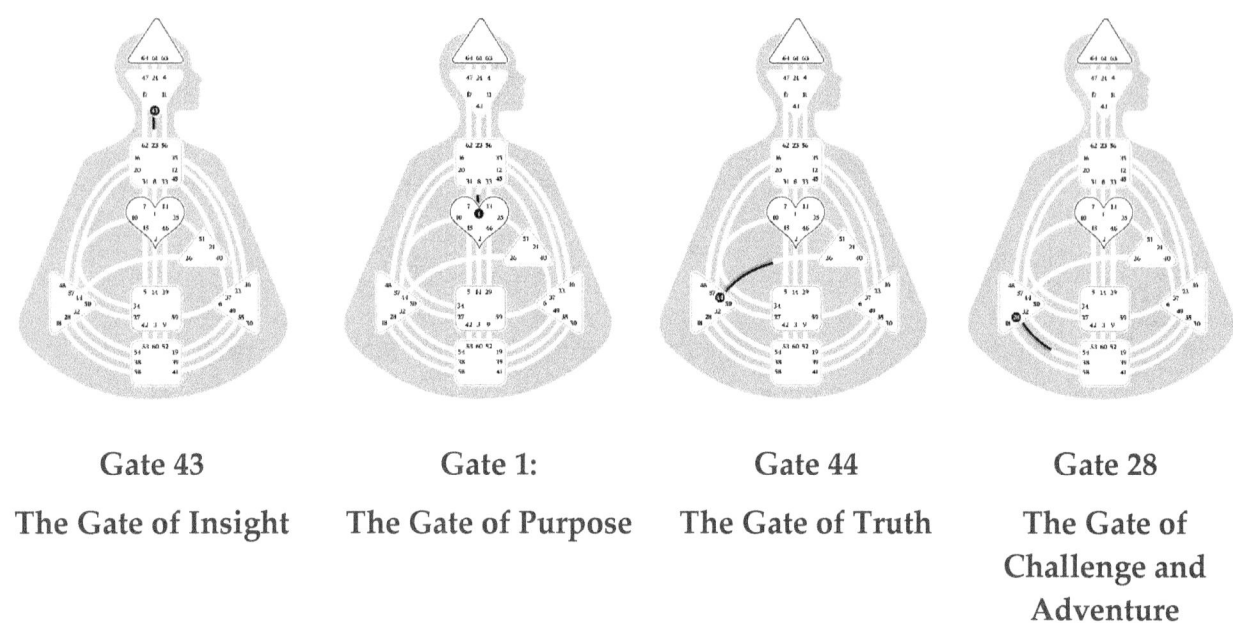

Gate 43	Gate 1:	Gate 44	Gate 28
The Gate of Insight	The Gate of Purpose	The Gate of Truth	The Gate of Challenge and Adventure

Retrograde cycles encourage us to go inward to explore the themes the planets give us. Mercury is the planet associated with communication. When Mercury goes retrograde, it gives us an opportunity to go inward and contemplate how we can better align ourselves to have greater influence and impact in the world. Take your time to find the right words during this cycle. Do your best to not make big decisions, sign contracts, or make large purchases. Expect delays. Breathe and be patient with others (and yourself)!

During this Mercury retrograde cycle, as Mercury moves through Gate 43 (Insight), Gate 1 (Purpose), Gate 44 (Truth), and Gate 28 (Challenge and Adventure), we are invited into a deep reclamation of self. The overarching theme is radical, relentless authenticity. This is a powerful opportunity to reframe the past—not by bypassing the pain or difficulty but by transforming our relationship to it. The struggles, challenges, and patterns that once made us doubt our worth are no longer meant to define us. Instead, they become the soil from which our most purposeful self-expression can rise.

We are called to trust our inner knowing—to recognize that the thoughts we have and the truths we carry are not only valid, but essential. They are the raw material for crafting a deeply meaningful, aligned life, and for cultivating influence and sparking transformation in the world.

But this cycle also brings with it shadow. One shadow is the temptation to push ourselves outward in a way that is rebellious rather than aligned—to express from a place of proving instead of a place of knowing. When rebellion becomes a reaction to the past, rather than a healing of it, we risk creating more separation and struggle. Another shadow is frustration: the discomfort of not yet being able to fully articulate the changes we seek or the truth we carry. In that frustration, we may try to force timing, to push our insights prematurely into spaces or toward people who cannot yet see or value our brilliance.

This retrograde asks us to honor divine timing—to resist the urge to force clarity or recognition—and instead, to root deeply in our authenticity, trusting that when we align with our own truth, the right words, allies, and opportunities will emerge.

CHALLENGE:

The challenge of this Mercury retrograde cycle is the temptation to force radical, authentic self-expression before we've achieved true internal alignment—to speak or act from urgency, rebellion, or the need to prove, rather than from grounded knowing. At the same time, we may find ourselves trapped in the weight of the past, looping through old patterns, fears, and struggles so deeply that we begin to believe they're permanent and insurmountable. This can lead to a quiet resignation, a false belief that no matter what we do, authentic expression will always be just out of reach. To surmount this challenge, we must release and heal the patterns of the past and fully embrace all of who we are meant to be. Only then can our self-expression flow from alignment, clarity, and the deep truth of our purpose.

OPTIMAL EXPRESSION:

The optimal expression of this Mercury retrograde cycle is a courageous, experiential journey into authentic self-expression—earned not through perfection or certainty, but through trial, error, and deep inner reckoning. It invites us to explore the terrain of our past not as a trap but as a teacher. Through the bumps, missteps, and brave experiments in self-expression, we uncover what is truly aligned. This cycle asks us to stay curious in the face of challenge, to let every moment of resistance or frustration reveal where we are still healing, still calibrating, still becoming. It's a time to honor the messy beauty of growth—to speak even when our voice trembles, to show up even when the path is unclear, and to trust that through the process of living and learning we refine not only our voice but our purpose. Authenticity is not a fixed state—it is a practice of returning to ourselves again and again, more honest, more whole, and more aligned each time.

UNBALANCED EXPRESSION:

The unbalanced expression of this Mercury retrograde cycle shows up as reactive, ungrounded self-expression—speaking or acting from a place of rebellion, urgency, or the need to prove, rather than from clarity and alignment. It can also manifest as emotional hesitation, where fear of repeating past struggles leads to self-censorship, doubt, and disconnection from our truth. In this state, we may try to force insight or prematurely share our brilliance with people who can't see or value it, leading to further frustration and wounding. Without reflection and integration, the cycle becomes a loop of reaction instead of revelation, rebellion instead of healing, and expression without embodiment.

CONTEMPLATIONS:

- Where am I still trying to prove my worth instead of trusting it?
- What past stories or patterns still influence how I see myself—and are they true now?
- Am I allowing divine timing to guide my expression—or am I trying to force clarity or recognition?
- What does radical authenticity look and feel like in my life, and where am I still holding back?
- How can I transform my past challenges into wisdom that empowers my voice?

AFFIRMATION:

I honor the truth of who I am. I honor the power and the preciousness of my authentic self-expression. I share my voice and my heart with people who truly see me and my value. I release the patterns of the past and express myself with courage, clarity, and divine timing. My voice is rooted in purpose, and my authenticity is my greatest power.

OCTOBER 25, 2026

GATE 28: CHALLENGE AND ADVENTURE

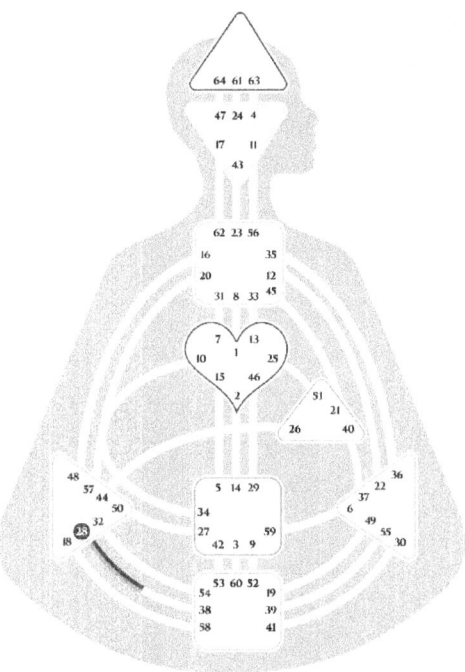

 **CHALLENGE:**

To not let struggle and challenge leave you feeling defeated and despairing. To learn to face life as an adventure. Do not let challenge and struggle cause you to feel as if you have failed.

 **AFFIRMATION:**

I am here to push the boundaries of life and what is possible. I thrive in situations that challenge me. I am an explorer on the leading edge of consciousness, and my job is to test how far I can go. I embrace challenge. I am an adventurer. I share all that I have learned from my challenges with the world. My stories help give people greater meaning, teach them what is truly worthy of creating, and inspire people to transform.

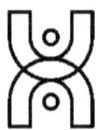

JOURNAL QUESTIONS:

- How can I turn my challenge into adventure?
- Where do I need to cultivate a sense of adventure in my life?
- What do I need to do to rewrite the story of my "failures"?
- What meanings, blessings, and lessons have I learned from my challenges?
- What needs to be healed, released, aligned, and brought to my awareness for me to trust myself and my choices?

What do I need to do to forgive myself for my perceived past failures?

EFT SETUP:

Even though everything feels hard, I now trust that I am learning what is truly important in my life. I trust the lessons the Universe brings me, and I deeply and completely love and accept myself.

EARTH:

Gate 27: Accountability

Are you taking responsibility for things that aren't yours to be responsible for? Whose problem is it? Can you return the responsibility for the problem back to its rightful owner?

OCTOBER 26, 2026

FULL MOON

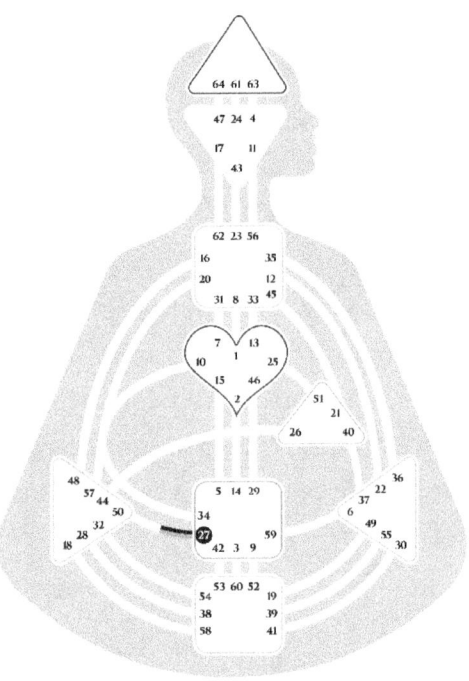

Taurus 2°45'

Gate 27: The Gate of Accountability

Full moon energy invites us to explore what we need to release and let go of in order to stay in alignment with our intentions.

The full moon on October 26, 2026, invites a profound clearing and realignment with your truth. Full moons illuminate what must be healed and released to make space for your fullest potential to emerge. This moon brings with it the energy of Gate 27, the Gate of Accountability in Quantum Human Design. It calls us to examine the structures of care, responsibility, and nourishment in our lives. Where have we overextended ourselves? Where have we taken on burdens that are not truly ours to carry? This is an opportunity to release distorted patterns of caretaking, obligation, and self-sacrifice that drain your life force and distract you from your own evolution.

In the shadow of Gate 27, we often find ourselves tangled in codependency, feeling responsible for the emotions, outcomes, and choices of others. This can manifest as guilt, as a compulsion to fix things, or as chronic overgiving. When left unchecked, this pattern keeps us from stepping into our own power and truth. The full moon illuminates these dynamics and asks us to let go—of the guilt, of the stories, of the unspoken agreements that keep us overattached and under-resourced. True accountability is not about martyrdom; it is about discernment. It is about caring from a place of alignment, not depletion.

But this energy also asks an equally important question: Where are you avoiding your own responsibility? Have you become passive in your own life, waiting for someone else to lead, to save, to initiate change on your behalf? This moon shines a light on areas where you may have abdicated your authority, ignored your inner knowing, or dismissed your role in shaping your life's direction. There is deep medicine in reclaiming ownership—of your choices, your habits, your path. When you stop outsourcing your power and begin to walk in alignment with your personal integrity, you liberate yourself to live more fully and truthfully.

As this full moon rises, it brings with it the power to break old patterns and restore energetic balance. It offers a sacred invitation to clean up the agreements, obligations, and unconscious habits that no longer serve you. You are not here to carry the weight of the world, nor are you here to remain small and dependent. You are here to stand in truth, to care in integrity, and to act with clarity. Let this moon be a moment of radical realignment—with your responsibilities, your relationships, and your deepest sense of purpose.

CHALLENGE:

The big lesson of the October 26, 2026, full moon is discernment in responsibility—learning to distinguish between what is truly yours to carry and what is not. Under the influence of Gate 27, the Gate of Accountability, this moon teaches that real nourishment and sustainable care begin with alignment. It challenges you to release guilt, codependency, and the habit of overfunctioning for others, while also asking you to reclaim the areas where you've been underfunctioning in your own life. The essential wisdom here is that freedom and fulfillment come from taking sacred responsibility for your own path—and letting go of everything that blocks you from walking it with clarity, courage, and integrity.

OPTIMAL EXPRESSION:

The optimal experience of this full moon is one of liberation and clarity—a gentle yet powerful shedding of false responsibility and a deep return to self. It's a moment of recommitment to your own path, where you release the burdens that don't belong to you and step more fully into aligned, empowered care for yourself and your purpose. This full moon offers the grace to nourish what truly matters and let go of what no longer does.

UNBALANCED EXPRESSION:

An unbalanced expression of this full moon might show up as heightened guilt, burnout, or resentment from overgiving and feeling responsible for everyone else's well-being. You may feel triggered by unmet expectations or tempted to control others in an attempt to fix what's not yours to fix. Alternatively, you might avoid responsibility altogether, deflecting ownership of your choices and relying on others to carry the weight of your life.

CONTEMPLATIONS:

- What responsibilities am I currently carrying that may not actually belong to me?
- Where in my life do I feel guilt or obligation, and is that energy rooted in truth or in fear?
- In what ways have I been overgiving or overfunctioning in my relationships, and what is it costing me?
- Are there areas of my life where I've stepped back from my own accountability or allowed others to make choices I need to own?
- What would it feel like to care for myself and others from a place of alignment rather than depletion?

AFFIRMATION:

I release what is not mine to carry and reclaim full responsibility for my own path. I nourish myself with truth, set clear boundaries with love, and walk forward in integrity and aligned care.

OCTOBER 31, 2026

GATE 44: TRUTH

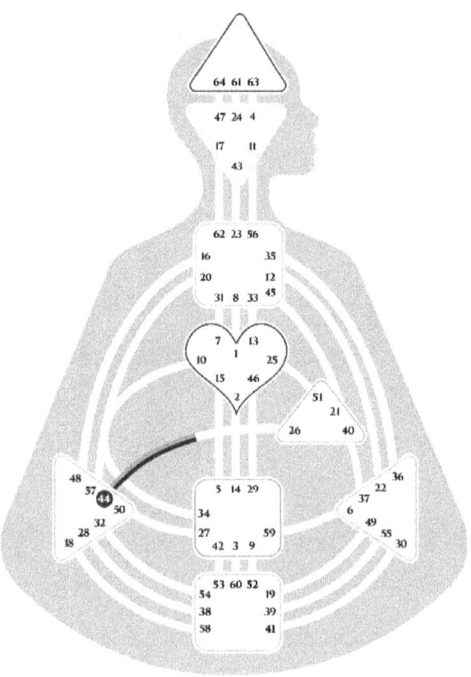

CHALLENGE:

To not get stuck in past patterns. To cultivate the courage to go forward without being stuck in the fear of the past. To learn how to transform pain into power and to have the courage to express your authentic self without compromising or settling.

AFFIRMATION:

I am powerfully intuitive and can sense the patterns that keep others stuck in limiting beliefs and constricted action. Through my insights and awareness, I help others break free from past limiting patterns and learn to find the power in their pain, find the blessings in their challenges, and align more deeply with an authentic awareness of their true value and purpose.

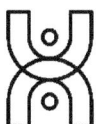
JOURNAL QUESTIONS:

- What patterns from the past are holding me back from moving forward with courage?
- Do I see how my experiences from the past have helped me learn more about who I truly am?
- What have I learned about my value and my power?
- What needs to be healed, released, aligned, and brought to my awareness for me to fully activate my power?
- What needs to be healed, released, aligned, and brought to my awareness for me to step boldly into my aligned and authentic path?

EFT SETUP:

Even though it is hard for me to let go, I deeply and completely love and accept myself. Even though I am afraid to repeat the past, I now move forward with confidence, trusting that I have learned what I needed to learn. I can create whatever future I desire, and I deeply and completely love and accept myself.

EARTH:

Gate 24: Blessings

Take some time to contemplate the hidden blessings in the painful events of the past. Can you find the bigger reason for why you've gone through what you've gone through?

NOVEMBER 6, 2026

GATE 1: PURPOSE

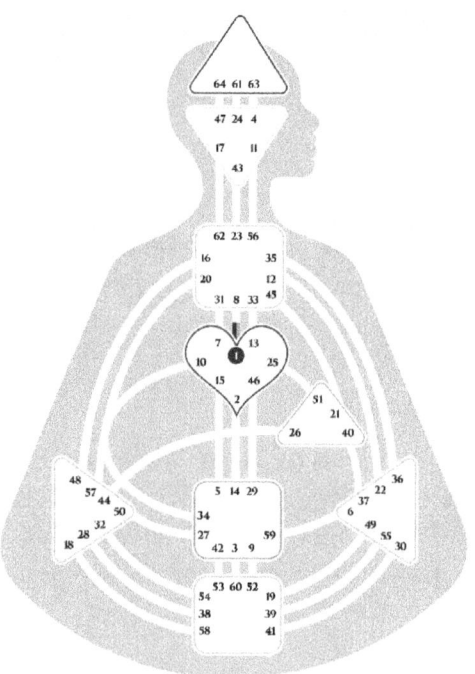

CHALLENGE:

To discover a personal, meaningful, and world-changing narrative that aligns with a sense of purpose and mission. "I am..." To learn to love yourself enough to honor the idea that your life is the canvas, and you are the artist. What you create with your life is the contribution you give the world.

AFFIRMATION:

My life is an integral part of the cosmos and the divine plan. I honor my life and know that the full expression of who I am is the purpose of my life. The more I am who I am, the more I create a frequency of energy that supports others in doing the same. I commit to exploring all of who I am.

JOURNAL QUESTIONS:
- Am I fully expressing my authentic self?
- What needs to be healed, released, aligned, or brought to my awareness for me to deeply express my authentic self?
- Where am I already expressing who I am?
- Where have I settled or compromised? What needs to change?
- Do I feel connected to my life purpose? What do I need to do to deepen that connection?

EFT SETUP:
Even though I am afraid that I am failing my life mission, I now choose to relax and allow my life to unfold before me with ease and grace. I trust that every step I take is perfectly aligned with my soul purpose, and I deeply and completely love and accept myself.

EARTH:
Gate 2: Allowing

How much good are you willing to allow into your life? Do you believe you can be fully supported?

NOVEMBER 9, 2026

NEW MOON

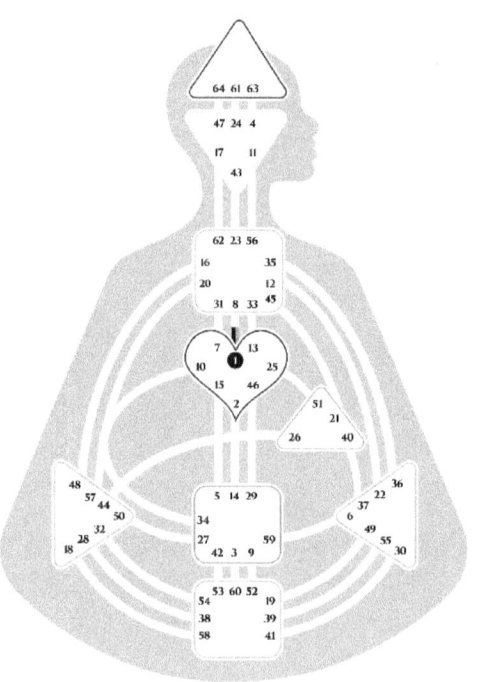

♏ Scorpio 16°52'

Gate 1: The Gate of Purpose

New moon energy invites us to explore how we can deepen our alignment with our intentions and asks us to focus on what we want to grow and expand on in our lives.

The November 9, 2026, new moon offers a potent opportunity to seed a new cycle of radical authenticity and creative self-expression. As with all new moons, this is a time of renewal, of planting new intentions and aligning with fresh possibilities. But this particular moon carries a deeper invitation—one rooted not in doing but in being. Gate 1, the Gate of Purpose in Quantum Human Design, reminds us that the foundation for meaningful expansion is not found in effort or hustle but in the courage to align with who we truly are.

Gate 1 is the most yang of all the hexagrams in the I'Ching—a creative force brimming with potential. Yet paradoxically, in the Human Design chart, it lives in the Calibration Center (traditionally the G Center), which holds no energy for action. Instead, this center governs identity, direction, and love. It teaches us that purpose doesn't arise from doing more but from becoming more—more truthful, more transparent, more aligned with our essential self. This gate calls forth a fierce commitment to authenticity and instructs us to build our life from the inside out.

The story we tell about who we are becomes the blueprint for how our lives unfold. The Gate of Purpose reminds us that if we calibrate our identity around fear, conditioning, or the pressure to conform, we will attract experiences that reinforce those distortions. But if we live from the story of our wholeness—if we express ourselves without compromise and take direction from our true essence—then the external world begins to reflect that coherence back to us. In this way, our alignment becomes magnetic, shaping the people, opportunities, and experiences that match our frequency.

This new moon is not a time for forcing things into form but for clarifying who you are becoming and embodying that identity with devotion. Your purpose is not a task to complete—it is a state of being to embody. This moon offers a reset, a return to the truth of who you are, and an invitation to allow your identity—not your effort—to shape the next chapter. This is the beginning of a new creative cycle, born not from striving but from alignment.

CHALLENGE:

The lesson of this new moon is that authentic alignment is the true source of purpose and creative power. When you embody the truth of who you are—without compromise—you naturally attract the people, paths, and possibilities that reflect your inner wholeness. Purpose isn't something you chase; it's something you become.

OPTIMAL EXPRESSION:

The optimal expression of this new moon is a bold, uncompromising alignment with your true identity—living and creating from the inside out. It's a time to trust that your authenticity is enough, and that your unique essence is the blueprint for your direction and impact. When you root into who you truly are, your life begins to flow with purpose, clarity, and creative momentum.

UNBALANCED EXPRESSION:

The unbalanced experience of this new moon may show up as self-doubt, creative hesitation, or the urge to conform in order to feel safe or accepted. You may feel disconnected from your sense of direction, seeking purpose through external validation rather than inner alignment. This imbalance can lead to frustration or a sense of aimlessness, as your actions no longer reflect the truth of who you are.

CONTEMPLATIONS:

- Where in my life am I compromising my authenticity for the sake of acceptance, safety, or success?
- What story am I currently telling about who I am—and is it aligned with the person I'm becoming?
- If I trusted that my purpose is already within me, how would I live differently today?
- What does it feel like in my body and heart when I am fully aligned with my true self?
- What one bold act of self-expression or truth-telling could I take now to anchor this new beginning?

AFFIRMATION:

I align with the truth of who I am and allow my authenticity to shape the path before me. My purpose unfolds effortlessly as I embody my essence with courage, clarity, and creative trust.

NOVEMBER 11, 2026

GATE 43: INSIGHT

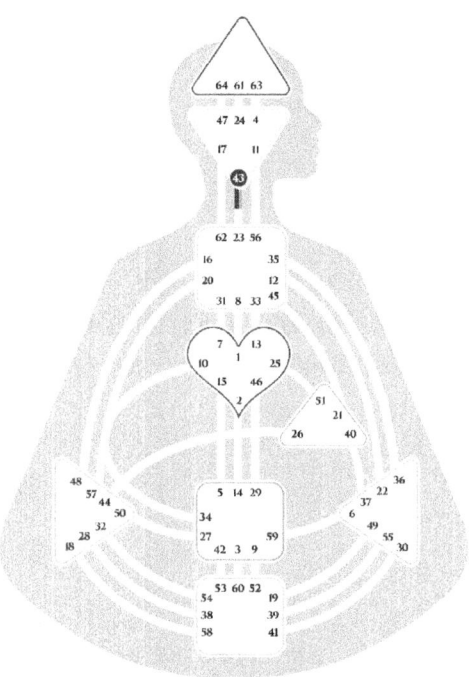

CHALLENGE:
To be comfortable and to trust epiphanies and deep inner knowing without doubting what you know. To trust that when the timing is right you will know how to share what you know and serve your role as a transformative messenger who has insights that can change the way people think and what they know.

AFFIRMATION:
I am a vessel of knowledge and wisdom that has the ability to transform the way people think. I share my knowledge with others when they are ready and vibrationally aligned with what I have to share. When the time is right, I have the right words and the right insights to help others expand their thinking, recalibrate their mindset, and discover the elegant solutions to the challenges facing humanity.

JOURNAL QUESTIONS:
- Do I trust in divine timing?
- Do I trust myself and my own inner knowing?
- What can I do to deepen my connection with my source of knowing?
- What needs to be healed, released, aligned, or brought to my awareness for me to trust my own inner knowing?

EFT SETUP:
Even though it is hard to wait for someone to ask me for my insights, I now choose to wait and know that my thoughts are valuable and precious. I only share them with people who value my insights, and I deeply and completely love and accept myself.

EARTH:
Gate 23: Transmission

Take stock of all the times you knew something even though you didn't know how you knew. Keep a running list of all your intuitive hits. Start affirming for yourself how reliable your knowingness is.

NOVEMBER 17, 2026

GATE 14: CREATION

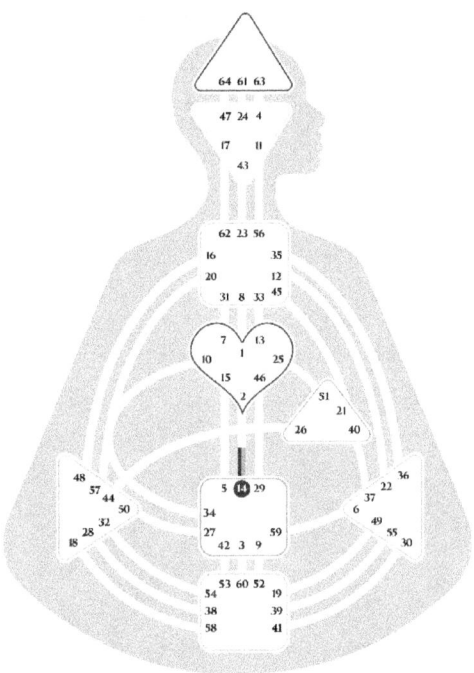

CHALLENGE:

To respond to opportunities that bring resources instead of forcing them or overworking. To learn to value resources and to appreciate how easily they can be created when you are aligned. To be gracious and grateful and not take for granted the resources you have.

AFFIRMATION:

I am in the flow of divine support. When I trust the generous nature of the Divine and I cultivate a state of faith, I receive all the opportunities and support that I need to evolve my life and transform the world. I know that the right work shows up for me, and I am fulfilled in the expression of my life-force energy.

JOURNAL QUESTIONS:
- Do I trust that I am supported?
- Am I doing my right work?
- What is the work that feels aligned with my purpose?
- How is that work showing up in my life right now?
- What resources do I have right now that I need to be grateful for?
- If I didn't need the money, what work would I be doing?

EFT SETUP:
Even though I am afraid that I cannot do what I love and make money, I deeply and completely love and accept myself.

EARTH:
Gate 8: Fulfillment

What would your life be like if you felt relentlessly authentic? Do one thing this week that is an authentic expression of who you are, without apology. Be bold.

NOVEMBER 22, 2026

GATE 34: POWER

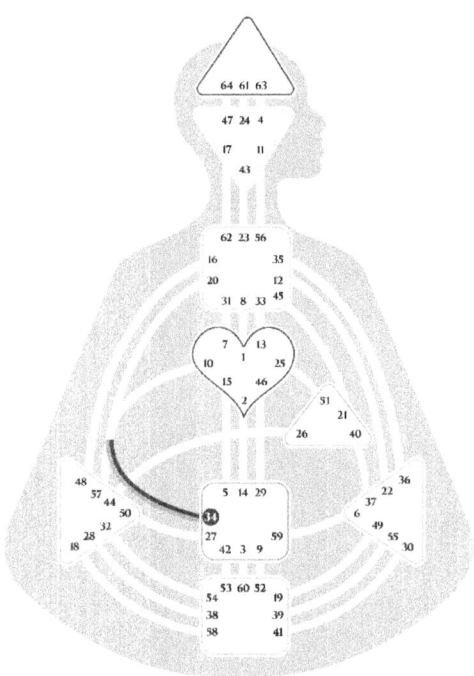

CHALLENGE:

To learn to measure out energy in order to stay occupied and busy but to not burn yourself out trying to force the timing or the rightness of a project. To wait to know which project or creation to implement based on when you get something to respond to.

AFFIRMATION:

I am a powerful servant of divine timing. When the timing is right, I unify the right people around the right idea and create transformation on the planet. My power is more active when I allow the Universe to set the timing. I wait. I am patient. I trust.

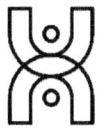

JOURNAL QUESTIONS:

- Do I trust in divine timing?

- What do I need to do to deepen my trust?
- How do I cultivate greater patience in my life?
- What fears come up for me when I think of waiting?
- How can I learn to wait with greater faith and ease?
- What do I do to occupy myself while I'm waiting?

EFT SETUP:

Even though I am afraid to be powerful, I now choose to fully step into my power and allow the Universe to serve me while I serve it, and I deeply and completely love and accept myself.

EARTH:

Gate 20: Patience

How do you manage the pressure you feel around the need for action? What are constructive ways that you can bring yourself into harmony with right timing? What do you do while you're waiting for the timing to align?

NOVEMBER 24, 2026

FULL MOON

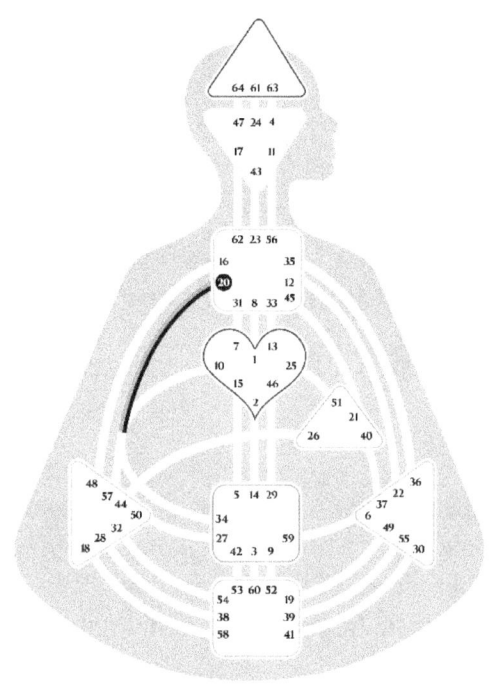

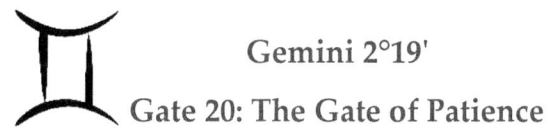 Gemini 2°19'
Gate 20: The Gate of Patience

Full moon energy invites us to explore what we need to release and let go of to stay in alignment with our intentions.

The full moon on November 24, 2026, illuminates the energy of Gate 20, the Gate of Patience. Full moons are always a time of heightened awareness, offering us an opportunity to release what no longer serves us and to align more deeply with our authentic potential. This particular full moon highlights the importance of divine timing and the wisdom of restraint. Gate 20, located in the Activation Center (Throat Center), teaches us that while we may feel the urgency to express, act, or respond, real power comes from waiting until the moment is truly right.

Gate 20 regulates some of the most influential energies in the Human Design chart: Gate 10, the Gate of Self-Love; Gate 57, the Gate of Instinct; and Gate 34, the Gate of Power. These gates together weave a matrix of deeply intuitive self-expression and aligned action, but none of their gifts can be fully accessed or expressed without the patient awareness of Gate 20. It reminds us that we are not in control of timing—we are stewards of preparation. Our role is not to force the unfolding but to stay devoted to our readiness and alignment, trusting that the moment to speak or act will arrive with clarity and resonance.

In this full moon light, we're called to examine how we're using our voice and our energy. Are we pushing to be heard or recognized in places where we're not truly received? Are we speaking before we're fully aligned or before our audience is ready? Are we acting out of impatience or urgency instead of grounded clarity? This moon offers us the chance to release the pressure to make things happen and instead trust in the synchrony that unfolds when our preparation meets divine timing.

Ultimately, this is a moon of vocal refinement and energetic maturity. It challenges us to become wise keepers of our power—conscious of when, where, and how we share our gifts, words, and insights. When we honor timing, the voice becomes a sacred instrument that can heal, lead, and inspire with precision. This full moon invites you to pause, recalibrate your relationship to timing, and recommit to the sacred art of speaking—and acting—only when the moment is truly right.

CHALLENGE:

The big lesson of this full moon is that true power lies in patience and timing. We are not here to force outcomes but to cultivate alignment, trust our inner knowing, and wait for the right moment to speak and act. When we do, our words and energy become catalysts for love, healing, and meaningful transformation.

OPTIMAL EXPRESSION:

The optimal experience of this full moon energy is one of peaceful alignment, where you feel grounded in your worth and attuned to the rhythm of divine timing. Rather than striving or pushing, you speak and act from a place of inner clarity and trust, knowing that your presence and voice have impact when shared in the right moment. This creates a sense of ease, flow, and empowered connection with both yourself and others.

UNBALANCED EXPRESSION:

The unbalanced experience of this full moon might feel like urgency, frustration, or pressure to be seen, heard, or take action before the moment is ripe. You may find yourself oversharing, pushing your wisdom onto unreceptive audiences, or doubting your value when external recognition is lacking. This can lead to burnout, miscommunication, or a sense of disconnection from your true power.

CONTEMPLATIONS:

- Where in my life am I trying to force timing, rather than trusting that the right moment will reveal itself naturally?

- What wisdom or truth within me is ready to be expressed—but only when the audience and timing are fully aligned?

- In what situations do I feel unseen, unheard, or undervalued, and what might shift if I waited for resonance rather than recognition?

- How can I better honor the sacred power of my voice by speaking with intention, clarity, and presence?

- What practices or choices help me stay grounded and patient, even when I feel the pressure to act or speak before I'm fully ready?

AFFIRMATION:

I trust the timing of my life and honor the power of my voice by speaking only when alignment calls. My words are sacred, my presence is purposeful, and I release the need to rush what is unfolding with perfect wisdom.

NOVEMBER 28, 2026

GATE 9: CONVERGENCE

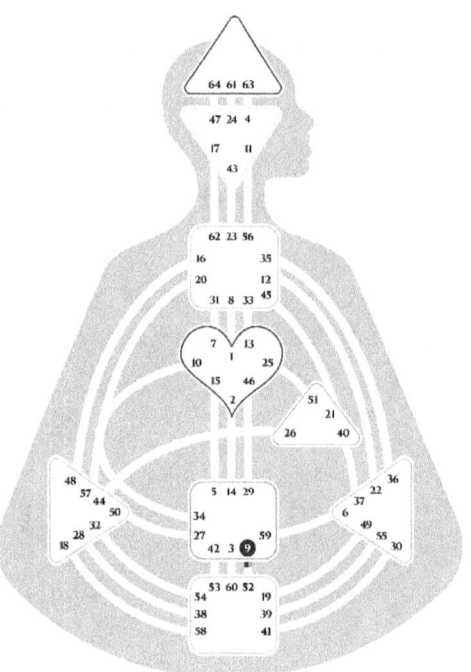

CHALLENGE:

The energy is about learning where to place your focus. When we work with the energy of this Gate, we have to learn to see the trees and the forest. This gate can make us seem unaware of the big picture, and we can lose our focus by getting stuck going down a rabbit hole.

AFFIRMATION:

I place my focus and attention on the details that support my creative manifestation. I am clear. I easily see the parts of the whole, and I know exactly what to focus on to support my evolution and the evolution of the world.

JOURNAL QUESTIONS:

- Where am I putting my energy and attention? Is it creating the growth that I am seeking?
- What do I need to focus on?
- Is my physical environment supporting my staying focused?
- Do I have a practice that supports my sustaining my focus? What can I do to increase my focus?

EFT SETUP:

Even though I have been frustrated with my lack of focus, I now choose to be clear, stay focused, and take the actions necessary to create my intentions.

EARTH:

Gate 16: Zest

Where have you sidelined your enthusiasm because others have told you that you can't do what you dream of doing?

DECEMBER 4, 2026

GATE 5: CONSISTENCY

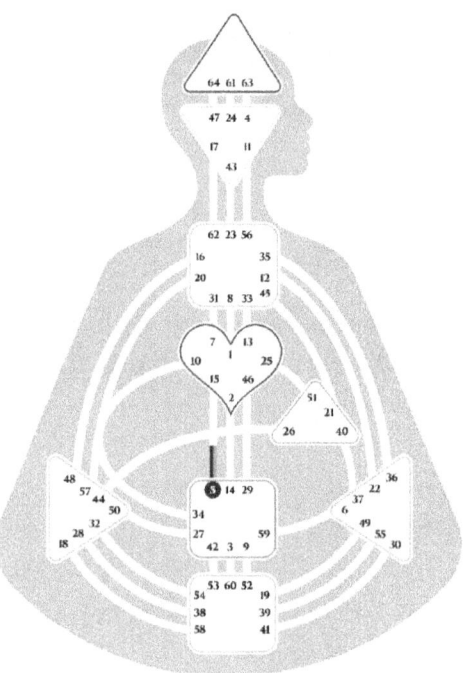

CHALLENGE:

To learn to craft order, habits, and rhythm that support alignment, connection, and the flow of life-force energy and the fulfillment of purpose. To become skilled at staying in tune with consistent habits and alignment that support your growth and evolution no matter what is going on around you. To align with natural order and stay attuned to the unfolding of the flow of the natural world.

AFFIRMATION:

Consistency gives me power. When I am aligned with my own natural rhythm and the rhythm of life around me, I cultivate strength and connection with Source, and I am a beacon of stability and order. The order I hold is the touchstone, the returning point of love, that is sustained through cycles of change. The rhythms I maintain set the standard for compassionate action in the world.

JOURNAL QUESTIONS:

- What do I need to do to create habits that fuel my energy and keep me vital and feeling connected to myself and Source?
- What habits do I have that might not be serving my highest expression? How can I change those habits?
- What kind of environment do I need to cultivate to support my rhythmic nature?

EFT SETUP:

Even though I feel nervous, scared, or worried about waiting for divine timing, I now choose to create habits that support my connection with Source while I wait, and I deeply and completely love and accept myself.

EARTH:

Gate 35: Experience

What experiences and stories from your own life do you have to share with others? Write a story about one of your favorite adventures. What did you learn? How has that shaped who you are?

DECEMBER 9, 2026

NEW MOON

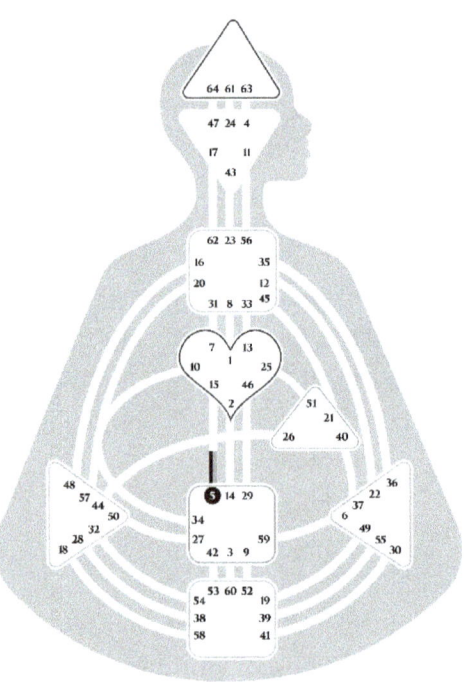

Sagittarius 16°56'

Gate 5: The Gate of Consistency

New moon energy invites us to explore how we can deepen our alignment with our intentions and asks us to focus on what we want to grow and expand on in our lives.

The December 9, 2026, new moon invites us to begin again—not just with intentions, but with the structure and devotion needed to sustain what we're building. New moon energy is always an opportunity to recalibrate and redirect our creative path, to seed new beginnings that will take root in the fertile dark. This particular new moon highlights Gate 5, the Gate of Consistency in Quantum Human Design, calling us to focus on the habits, rituals, and rhythms that support lasting growth. It reminds us that expansion is not just a product of effort but of aligned repetition—of showing up again and again for what we truly value.

Gate 5 holds the energy of timing, pattern, and sustainable practice. It is the frequency that allows us to create an inner and outer cadence that is reliable, grounding, and supportive. When we embrace its optimal expression, we are able to create sacred containers—habits that are infused with intention and aligned with our true desires. From this place, consistency becomes an act of devotion, not discipline. It becomes how we embody our dreams, one aligned action at a time.

In its shadow, this energy can amplify our struggle to maintain habits or feel productive, leading to shame, frustration, or even burnout. But inconsistency is not always a character flaw. More often than not, it's an indicator that we've been trying to maintain patterns that are misaligned with who we truly are or what we deeply desire. This new moon is not asking us to force ourselves into rigid routines. It is asking us to tell the truth about what we really want, and then build the kind of rhythm that honors that truth.

This is a moment to release the shame around what hasn't worked and to begin again—with integrity, clarity, and zero compromise. What daily, weekly, or seasonal patterns would actually support the life you are trying to create? What rituals would make you feel more rooted, more alive, more in sync with your own essence? The December new moon opens a doorway to pattern your reality around what truly matters. This is how we create the scaffolding that can hold our dreams—not just in theory but in practice.

CHALLENGE:

The core lesson of this new moon is that real growth requires rhythm—aligned, intentional consistency rooted in what truly matters to you. To optimize this energy, stop forcing yourself into patterns that don't fit and instead build daily practices that nourish your authentic dreams and prepare you for meaningful expansion.

OPTIMAL EXPRESSION:

The optimal experience of this new moon energy is a sense of grounded momentum where your daily habits feel purposeful, aligned, and supportive of your long-term vision. You feel connected to a rhythm that sustains you, not depletes you, and each small action becomes an act of devotion to the life you're consciously creating.

UNBALANCED EXPRESSION:

When this new moon energy is unbalanced, you may feel frustrated by your inability to stay consistent, caught in cycles of shame or self-judgment for not maintaining habits that may not even be right for you. Life can feel chaotic or stagnant as you push yourself to follow rhythms that don't align with your true nature. This imbalance is a signal to stop forcing and start listening—to cultivate patterns that nourish your becoming rather than control it.

CONTEMPLATIONS:

- What habits or patterns in my life currently feel life-giving, and which ones feel like

obligations disconnected from my true desires?
- Where am I mistaking force or discipline for alignment and devotion—and how can I shift into a more supportive rhythm?
- What daily or weekly practices would help me feel more grounded, purposeful, and prepared for growth?
- In what areas of my life do I crave consistency, and what would it look like to create that consistency in a way that honors my energy and truth?
- What am I ready to release—shame, unrealistic expectations, misaligned routines—so I can begin again with clarity and self-trust?

AFFIRMATION:

I create rhythms that honor my truth, build habits that nourish my becoming, and move in harmony with the timing of my soul.

DECEMBER 9, 2026

GATE 26: INTEGRITY

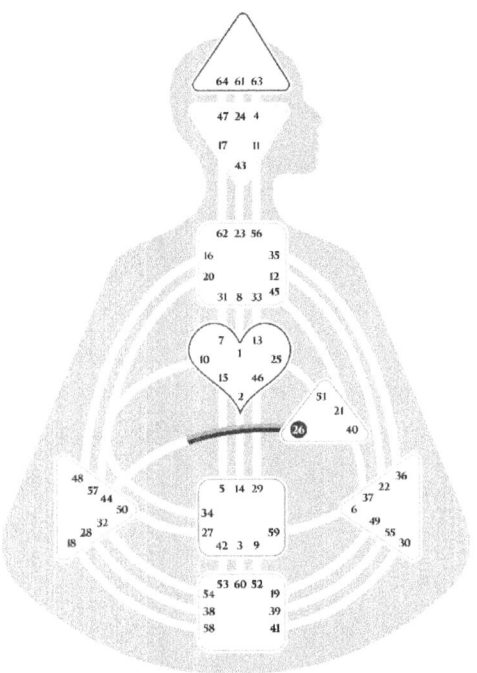

CHALLENGE:

To learn to value your right place and your value enough to act as if you are precious. To heal past traumas and elevate your self-worth. To trust in support enough to do the right thing and to nurture yourself so that you have more to give.

AFFIRMATION:

I am a unique, valuable, and irreplaceable part of the cosmic plan. I am always supported in fulfilling my right place. I take care of my body, my energy, my values, and my resources so that I have more to share with the world. I claim and defend my value and fully live in the story of who I am with courage.

JOURNAL QUESTIONS:
- Where might I be experiencing a breach in my moral identity or my physical, resource, or energy integrity?
- What do I need to do to bring myself back into integrity?
- When I act without integrity, can it be traumatic?
- What trauma do I have that I need to heal?
- How can I rewrite that story of my trauma as an initiation back into my true value?
- What do I need to do right now to nurture myself and to replenish my value?

EFT SETUP:
Even though I am afraid to share my truth, I now choose to speak my truth clearly and confidently, and I deeply and completely love and accept myself.

EARTH:
Gate 45: Distribution

This is a vital week to focus on what gifts you have to share with the world. How can you learn to give more without burning yourself out or martyring yourself? What do you need to do to increase your capacity to give and share?

DECEMBER 15, 2026

GATE 11: THE CONCEPTUALIST

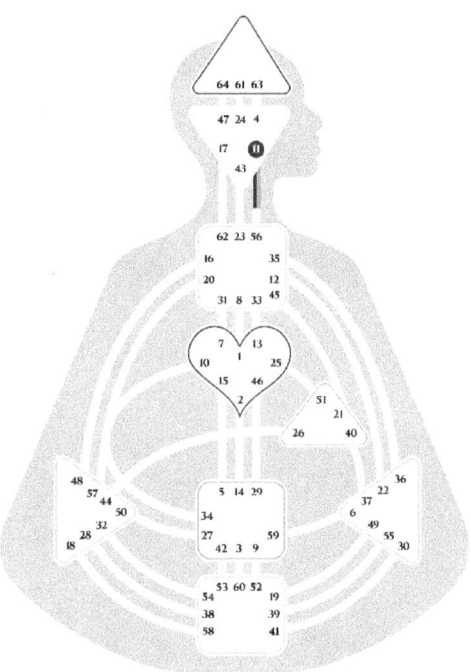

CHALLENGE:

To sort through and manage all the ideas and inspiration you hold. To trust that the ideas that are yours will show up for you in an actionable way. To value yourself enough to value the ideas you have and to wait for the right people to share those ideas with.

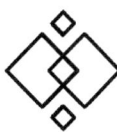

AFFIRMATION:

I am a divine vessel of inspiration. Ideas flow to me constantly. I protect and nurture these ideas, knowing that my purpose in life is to share ideas and inspiration with others. I use the power of these ideas to stimulate my imagination and the imagination of others. I trust the infinite abundance and alignment of the Universe, and I wait for signs to know which ideas are mine to manifest.

JOURNAL QUESTIONS:
- What do I do with inspiration when I receive it?
- Do I know how to serve as a steward for my ideas? Or do I feel pressure to try to force them into form?
- How much do I value myself? Am I valuing my ideas?
- Do I trust the Universe? Do I trust that the ideas that are mine to take action on will manifest in my life according to my Human Design Type and Strategy?
- What can I do to manage the pressure I feel to manifest my ideas?
- Am I trying to prove my value with my ideas?

EFT SETUP:
Even though I have so many ideas, I now trust that I will know exactly what action to take and when to take it, and I deeply and completely love and accept myself.

EARTH:
Gate 12: The Channel

Spend some time this week contemplating what you need to do to deepen your connection with Source. Add some kind of creativity to your play and rest this week.

DECEMBER 20, 2026

GATE 10: SELF-LOVE

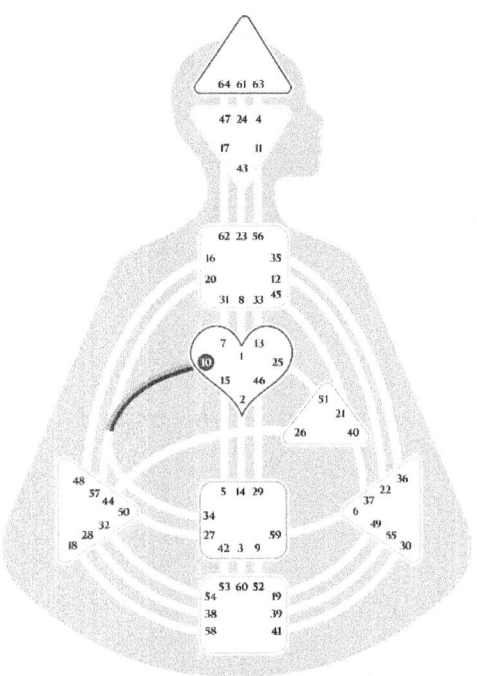

CHALLENGE:

To learn to love yourself. To learn to take responsibility for your own creations.

AFFIRMATION:

I am an individuated aspect of the Divine. I am born of love. My nature is to love and be loved. I am in the full flow of giving and receiving love. I know that the quality of love that I have for myself sets the direction for what I attract into my life. I am constantly increasing the quality of love I experience and share with the world.

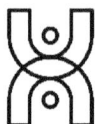

JOURNAL QUESTIONS:

- Do I love myself?
- What can I do to deepen my self-love?
- Where can I find evidence of my lovability in my life right now?
- What do I need to do to take responsibility for situations I hate in my life right now? What needs to change?
- Where am I holding blame or victimhood in my life? How could I turn that energy around?

EFT SETUP:

Even though I struggle with loving myself, I now choose to be open to discovering how to love myself anyway, and I deeply and completely love and accept myself.

EARTH:

Gate 15: Compassion

Contemplate what old patterns in your life right now need to be healed and released. Take at least one grounded or symbolic way to commit to shifting and changing these patterns.

DECEMBER 24, 2026

FULL MOON

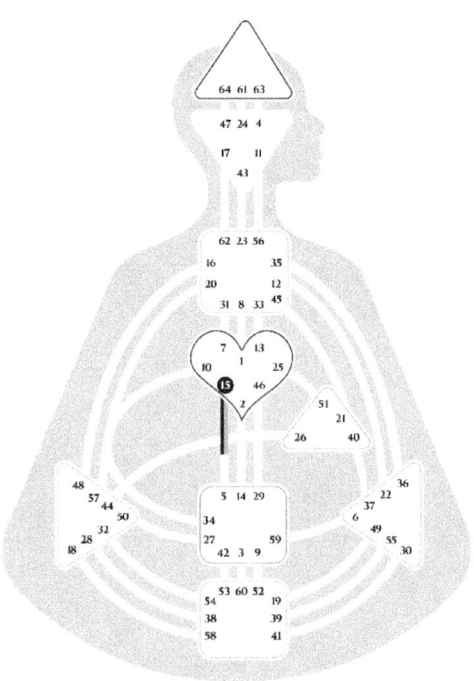

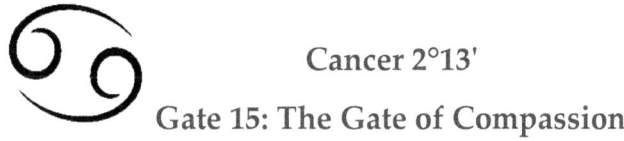

Cancer 2°13'

Gate 15: The Gate of Compassion

Full moon energy invites us to explore what we need to release and let go of to stay in alignment with our intentions.

The final full moon of 2026 arrives on December 24, shining a radiant light on Gate 15, the Gate of Compassion in Quantum Human Design. Full moons are always moments of illumination, revealing what must be healed, released, aligned, or acknowledged for us to grow into the next evolution of ourselves. As the calendar year closes, this full moon offers us a powerful moment of reflection. We're invited to look back at the choices, patterns, and energies we've carried this year and decide what is worthy of bringing into the next cycle—and what is ready to be transmuted.

Gate 15 is deeply tied to the energy of compassion, especially compassion expressed through sharing, generosity, and a willingness to be in rhythm with the world around us. This is a heart-centered time to reflect on how we've used our abundance—not just materially, but energetically, emotionally, and spiritually. Have we hoarded our gifts or shared them freely? Have we honored the humanity in others as much as we've worked to align with our own truth? Compassion asks us not only to care but to act on that care in real and tangible ways that increase the collective good.

In resonance with the energy of the preceding new moon in Gate 5, which asked us to build new habits and patterns that support long-term growth, this full moon now asks us to turn our gaze to what must be broken down. What no longer fits? What rhythms once served us but now stifle us? This is an invitation to release old routines, outdated consistency, and rigid schedules that are not rooted in joy or authenticity. Just as a forest fire clears away the old underbrush to make room for new life, we are being invited to clear energetic space in order to plant new seeds into the fertile ground of our own evolution.

This full moon is a sacred moment of both reckoning and blessing. As we release the old with compassion—toward ourselves and others—we create space for a new rhythm to emerge, one that is rooted in authenticity, generosity, and deeply aligned habits. We are not starting from scratch. We are beginning from wisdom. This wisdom, shaped by a year of lived experience, reveals to us what no longer needs to be carried and invites us to step forward into the next season lighter, clearer, and more rooted in the truth of who we really are.

CHALLENGE:

One of the key lessons of this full moon is learning to harness extreme energy wisely. The shadow of Gate 15 can show up as engaging in extremes or misusing our energy and resources in unsustainable ways. We're reminded that extreme action has its place—not as a lifestyle, but as a catalyst to break free from outdated patterns and return to a more authentic rhythm.

OPTIMAL EXPRESSION:

The optimal expression of this energy is compassionate alignment with natural, authentic rhythms—both our own and those of the collective. It's the ability to flow with life while remaining grounded in our values, using our abundance to uplift others and create harmony. Rather than pushing through extremes, we cultivate sustainable practices that reflect generosity, consistency, and a deep respect for the interconnectedness of all things.

UNBALANCED EXPRESSION:

An unbalanced expression of this energy can show up as swinging between extremes—overgiving and burnout, rigidity and chaos, isolation and overimmersion in others' needs. It may manifest as using energy or resources recklessly, trying to force alignment through intensity rather than presence. In this state, we may either resist natural rhythms or attempt to control them, losing touch with compassion and the flow that Gate 15 is meant to embody.

CONTEMPLATIONS:

- Where in my life am I clinging to rhythms or routines that no longer support my authenticity or growth?
- How can I use my abundance—time, energy, resources—to bless others without depleting myself?
- In what ways have I allowed extremes to shape my patterns, and where might I now return to balance?
- What needs to be compassionately released for me to live more aligned with my truth?
- How can I cultivate daily practices that honor both my individuality and my connection to the collective?

AFFIRMATION:

I release what no longer serves with compassion and grace, aligning myself with rhythms that nourish my soul and uplift the world around me. My energy flows in harmony with purpose, presence, and love.

DECEMBER 26, 2026

GATE 58: THE GATE OF JOY

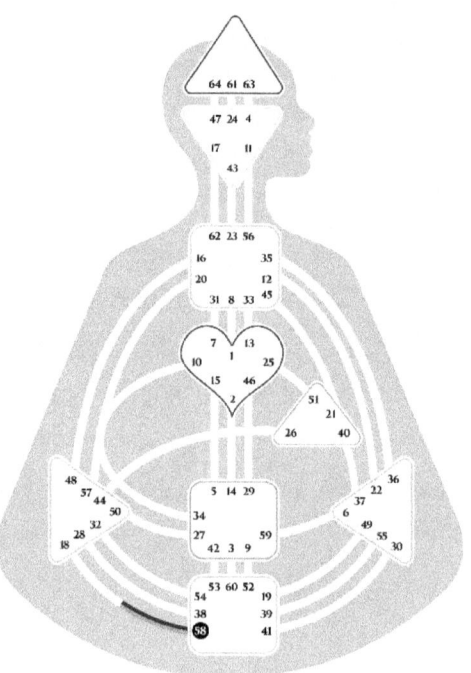

CHALLENGE:

To follow the drive to create the fulfillment of your potential. To learn to craft a talent and make it consummate through joyful learning and repetition. To learn to embrace joy as a vital force of creative power without guilt or denial.

AFFIRMATION:

I am a consummate curator of my own talent. I use my joy to drive me to embody the fun expression of all that I am. I practice as my path to excellency. I know that from repetition and consistency comes a more skillful expression of my talent. I embrace learning and growing, and I commit to the full expression of my joy.

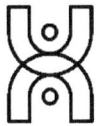
JOURNAL QUESTIONS:
- What brings me the greatest joy?
- How can I deepen my practice of joy?
- How can I create more joy in my life?
- What keeps me from fulfilling my potential and my talent?
- What am I afraid of?

EFT SETUP:
Even though it is hard to let go of the past, I now choose to release it and embrace all the joy that is available to me right now, and I deeply and completely love and accept myself.

EARTH:
Gate 52: Perspective

Is there anything in your environment or your life that you need to move out of the way for you to deepen your focus?

DECEMBER 31, 2026

GATE 38: THE VISIONARY

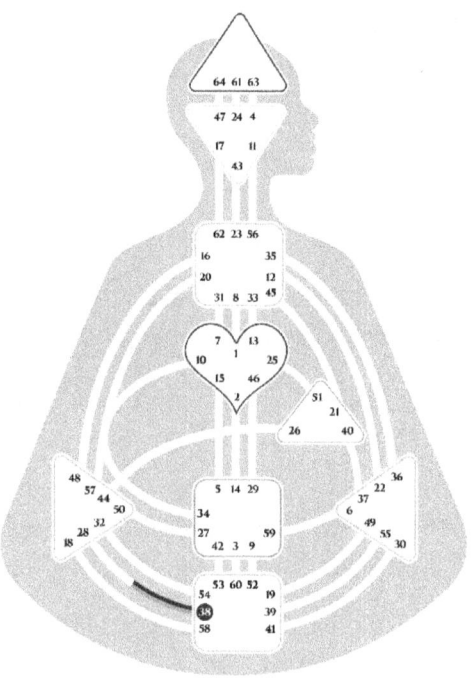

CHALLENGE:
To experience challenge as a way of knowing what is worth fighting for. To turn the story of struggle into a discovery of meaning and to let the power of what you discover serve as a foundation for a strong vision of transformation that brings dreams into manifested form.

AFFIRMATION:
My challenges, struggles, and adventures have taught me about what is truly valuable in life. I use my understandings to hold a vision of what else is possible for the world. I am aligned with the values that reflect the preciousness of life, and I sustain a vision for a world that is aligned with heart. My steadfast commitment to my vision inspires others to join me in creating a world of equitable, sustainable peace.

JOURNAL QUESTIONS:
- Do I know what is worth committing to and fighting for in my life?
- Do I have a dream that I am sharing with the world?
- Do I know how to use my struggles and challenges as the catalyst for creating deeper meaning in the world? In my life?

EFT SETUP:
Even though things seem hard and challenging, I now choose to use my challenges to help me get clear about what I really want, and I deeply and completely love and accept myself.

EARTH:
Gate 39: Recalibration

Where do you need to tweak your perspective to see abundance where you think there is lack? How can you shift the story to see what you have versus what you think you don't? Spend some time practicing reframing your perspective this week.

JANUARY 6, 2027

GATE 54: DIVINE INSPIRATION

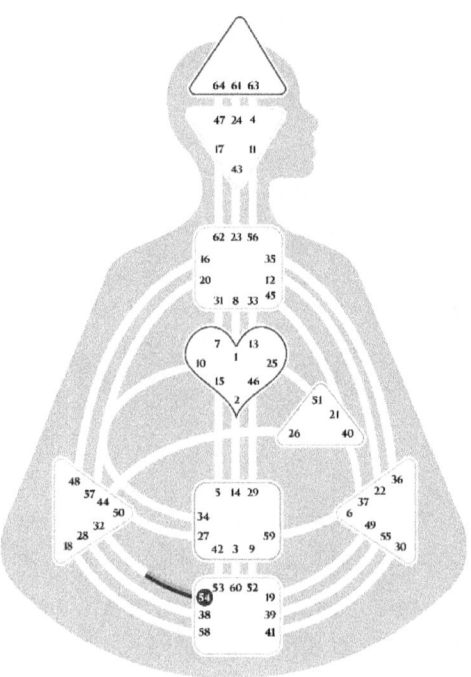

CHALLENGE:

To learn to be a conduit for divine inspiration. To be patient and to wait for alignment and right timing before taking action. To be at peace with stewardship for ideas and to learn to trust the divine trajectory of an inspiration.

AFFIRMATION:

I am a divine conduit for inspiration. Through me new ideas about creating sustainability and peace on the planet are born. I tend to my inspirations, give them love and energy, and prepare the way for their manifestations in the material world.

JOURNAL QUESTIONS:

- What do I do to get inspired?
- How do I interface with my creative muse?
- Is there anything I need to do or prepare to be ready for the next step in the manifestation of my dream or inspiration?
- How will I know when I am inspired? Will I feel it in my body?

EFT SETUP:

Even though I am afraid my dreams will not come true, I now choose to dream wildly and trust that my dreams will come true. All I have to do is focus my mind, trust, and know that all will unfold perfectly, and I deeply and completely love and accept myself.

EARTH:

Gate 53: Starting

What identities and attachments do you have about being the one who starts and finishes something? How can you deepen your trust in right timing?

JANUARY 7, 2027

NEW MOON

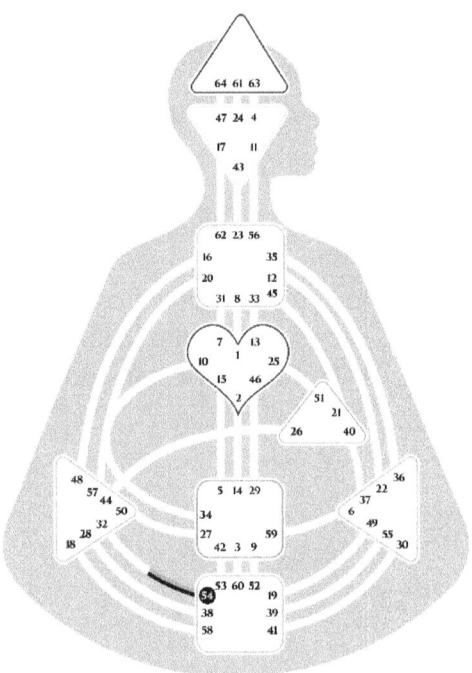

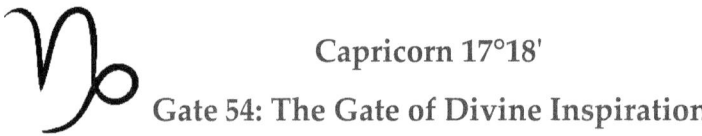 **Capricorn 17°18'**

Gate 54: The Gate of Divine Inspiration

New moon energy invites us to explore how we can deepen our alignment with our intentions and asks us to focus on what we want to grow and expand on in our lives.

The January 7, 2027, new moon arrives at a potent threshold—marking both the first new moon of the calendar year and the final new moon of the Quantum Human Design year. This is a liminal time, a moment when we are standing between worlds. We're simultaneously releasing what no longer serves and preparing ourselves to plant the seeds of what wants to be born. New moons always invite us to begin again, but this one comes with a deeper layer of reflection, transition, and preparation. As the old cycle comes to a close, we are asked to consciously set the tone for the new creative season ahead.

This new moon activates Gate 54, the Gate of Divine Inspiration. This gate holds the raw, ascending energy of ambition—but not ambition for ego's sake. This is a sacred drive to align our desires with something higher, something rooted in purpose and contribution. It is the divine spark that initiates movement, the inner voice that says, "It's time." In its highest expression, Gate 54 inspires us to take practical steps toward building a future that's infused with meaning and potential, all while remaining connected to Source. It reminds us that inspired ambition is not about grasping for success but about laying down foundations for sustainable and soul-aligned expansion.

However, the shadow of Gate 54 can trigger fear—fear that divine inspiration is temporary or fleeting. This fear can push us into urgency, competition, and scarcity. We may feel pressured to act fast, to chase the reward, to stake our claim before the opportunity disappears or someone else beats us to it. When this energy is misaligned, it becomes a race to the top without connection to the purpose behind the effort. We lose sight of the sacredness of the spark and instead become reactive, driven more by fear of loss than by trust in divine timing.

As this new moon bridges two energetic years, we are called to approach our beginnings with intentionality, patience, and trust. Let the inspiration rise. Let it settle. Ask yourself: What needs to be put in place now—internally and externally—so that I am ready to receive, build, and grow when the time comes? You don't need to rush or force. The spark is already within you. This new moon reminds us that true success begins with alignment and that when we root our dreams in inspiration and devotion, we prepare the ground for real and lasting transformation.

CHALLENGE:

The big lesson of this new moon is to trust the timing of divine inspiration and allow it to guide intentional, soul-rooted beginnings. Rather than rushing or reacting from fear of missing out, we're invited to lay steady, aligned foundations for future growth—knowing that what is truly ours will not pass us by.

OPTIMAL EXPRESSION:

The optimal expression of this new moon is inspired ambition rooted in purpose and divine alignment. It's a time to receive the spark of a new beginning, take grounded steps toward expansion, and prepare the structures that will support long-term, meaningful growth. When we move with trust and clarity, our efforts become sacred acts of creation.

UNBALANCED EXPRESSION:

The unbalanced expression of this new moon can show up as urgency, fear of missing out, and a push to act on inspiration without clarity or alignment. It may feel like a race to secure success before it slips away, leading to reactive decisions and burnout. This energy can disconnect us from trust and turn divine insight into anxious striving.

CONTEMPLATIONS:

- What inspired ideas are stirring within me right now, and how can I nurture them without rushing into action?
- Where am I being invited to build something of lasting value, and what foundational steps need to be put in place first?
- Am I acting from trust and alignment or from fear of missing out or being left behind?
- How can I strengthen my connection to Source so that my ambition stays rooted in purpose, not pressure?
- What structures, support systems, or practices can I commit to now to hold and sustain my next phase of growth?

AFFIRMATION:

I trust the divine timing of my inspiration. I root my ambition in purpose, align my actions with truth, and prepare the ground for sacred, sustainable growth.

JANUARY 11, 2027

GATE 61: WONDER

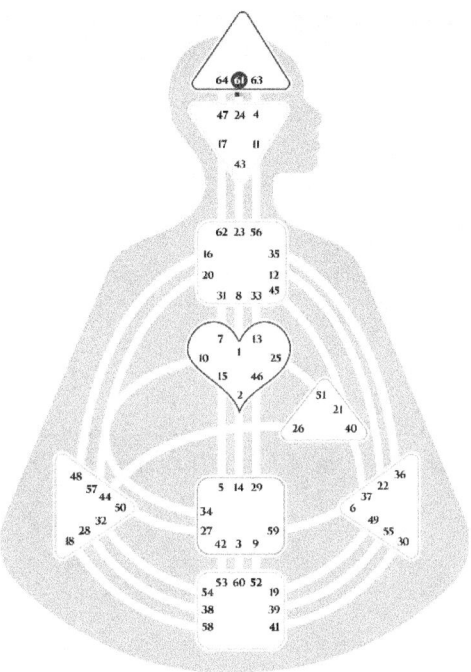

CHALLENGE:

To not get lost in trying to answer or figure out why. To maintain a state of wonder. To not let the pressure of trying to know keep you from being present.

AFFIRMATION:

I have a direct connection to a cosmic perspective that gives me an expanded view of the meaning of the events in my life and the lives of others. I see the wonder and innocence of life and stay present in a constant state of awe. I am innocent and pure in my understanding of the world, and my innocence is the source of my creative alignment.

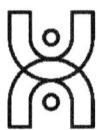

JOURNAL QUESTIONS:

- What do I do to maintain my sense of wonder?
- How can I deepen my awe of the magnificence of the Universe?
- What old thoughts, patterns, and beliefs do I need to release to align with my knowingness and to trust my "delusional confidence" as a powerful creative state?
- What greater perspectives on the events of my life can I see?
- What are the greatest lessons I've learned from my pain?
- How do I use these lessons to expand my self-expression?

EFT SETUP:

Even though I do not know all the answers, I now choose to surrender and trust that I am being loved, supported, and nurtured by the infinite loving Source that is the Universe.

EARTH:

Gate 62: Preparation

This week's mantra: I am prepared. I'll know what I need to know when I need to know it. I'll know what to prepare when it's time to prepare it. I relax and trust in the flow. Repeat as needed.

JANUARY 17, 2027

GATE 60: CONSERVATION

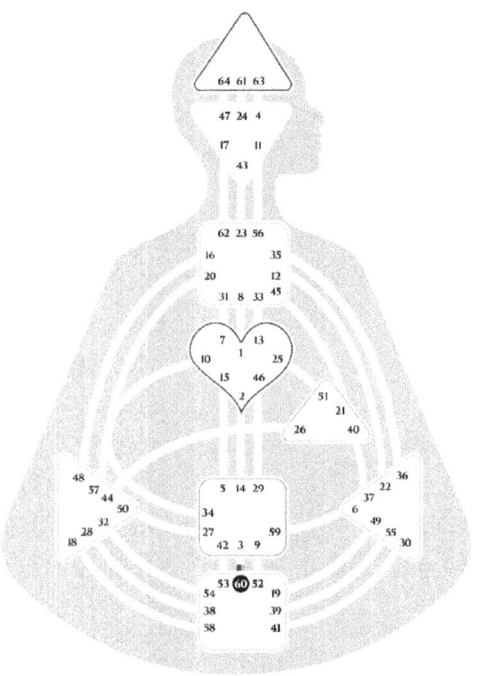

 **CHALLENGE:**

To not let the fear of loss overwhelm your resourcefulness. To learn to find what is working and focus on it instead of looking at the loss and disruption.

 **AFFIRMATION:**

I am grateful for all the transformation and change in my life. I know that disruption is the catalyst for my growth. I am able to find the blessings of the past and incorporate them in my innovative vision for the future. I am optimistic about the future, and I transform the world by growing what works.

JOURNAL QUESTIONS:
- What change am I resisting?
- What am I afraid of?
- What are the things in my life that are working and that I need to focus on?
- Is my fear of loss holding me back?

EFT SETUP:
Even though it is hard to let go of things that did not work, I now release all the clutter from the past, and I deeply and completely love, accept, and trust myself.

EARTH:
Gate 56: Expansion

Tell yourself a story about your life, your future, and your dreams that causes you to expand energetically. Allow yourself to truly fill up your energy field with expansion.

SUMMARY

Your Quantum Human Design is your key to understanding your energy, your life purpose, your life path, and your soul's journey in this lifetime. You are a once-in-a-lifetime cosmic event, and the fulfillment of your potential and purpose is the greatest gift you can give the world.

I hope this year has been revolutionary for you and that you reconnected with the true story of who you are and the power and possibility of your very special life.

If you need additional support and resources to help you on your life path and soul's journey, please visit quantumhumandesign.com, where you can find specialists and practitioners who will help you understand the story of your Human Design chart, coach you, and help you get to the root of any pain, blocks, or limiting beliefs that may be keeping you from enjoying your life story. There are all kinds of free goodies, videos, e-books, and resources to help you on your way!

Thank you again for being you! We are who we are because you are who you are!

From my Heart to Yours,

Dr. Karen

ABOUT THE AUTHOR

Dr. Karen Parker is an expert in Quantum Human Design and developed a system to help explore the relationship between quantum physics and Human Design. She's the creator of Quantum Conversations, a successful podcast with over 90,000 downloads in less than twelve months, and two systems of Human Design: Quantum Human Design and the Quantum Alignment System. Multiple news outlets, radio shows, and telesummits have featured her work on their programs.

Karen is also the author of numerous bestselling books all designed to help you create the life you were destined to live and find and embrace the purpose of your existence.

Karen is available for private consultations, keynote talks, and to conduct in-house seminars and workshops.

To run your chart with the new Quantum Human Design language,
go to freehumandesignchart.com and to find out more about Quantum Alignment visit this website: quantumhumandesign.com

You can reach her at Karen@quantumhumandesign.com.

For more great books on Human Design, please visit our online store at
books.gracepointpublishing.com

If you enjoyed reading *2026 Quantum Human Design Evolution Guide* and purchased it through an online retailer, please return to the site and write a review to help others find this book.

www.ingramcontent.com/pod-product-compliance
Lightning Source LLC
Chambersburg PA
CBHW060232240426
43671CB00016B/2916